The Governance of Sustainable Rural Renewal

This book examines examples of rural regeneration projects through the public administration lens, analysing how governance arrangements in rural settings work. In particular, the author focuses on the role of communities, business and tiers of governance (local, regional, national, and supra national) in terms of delivery and funding.

By drawing on a range of case studies from the UK, US, Australia and South Africa, the book identifies best practice in governance, applicable to both academic conceptual debates and to practitioners engaged in real-world governance of regeneration. While there are substantial political science, sociology and geography debates within the existing academic literature around food security, fair trade, urban–rural divides and supply chains, little has been written on the way in which governance in comparative global case study settings operates in achieving or underpinning rural renewal programmes.

Through the inclusion of dedicated sections in each chapter summarising the links between academic debate and practice, this book will be of great interest to researchers and policy-makers in the field of rural development, and environmental politics and governance in general.

Rory Shand is Senior Lecturer in Public Services at Manchester Metropolitan University, UK.

T0413634

Routledge Explorations in Environmental Studies

The Governance of Sustainable Rural Renewal

A comparative global perspective

Rory Shand

LONDON AND NEW YORK

First published 2016 by Routledge

2 Park Square, Milton Park, Abingdon, Oxfordshire OX14 4RN
711 Third Avenue, New York, NY 10017

Routledge is an imprint of the Taylor & Francis Group, an informa business

First issued in paperback 2017

© 2016 Rory Shand

The right of Rory Shand to be identified as author of this work has
been asserted by him in accordance with sections 77 and 78 of the
Copyright, Designs and Patents Act 1988.

All rights reserved. No part of this book may be reprinted or
reproduced or utilised in any form or by any electronic, mechanical,
or other means, now known or hereafter invented, including
photocopying and recording, or in any information storage or
retrieval system, without permission in writing from the publishers.

Trademark notice: Product or corporate names may be trademarks
or registered trademarks, and are used only for identification and
explanation without intent to infringe.

British Library Cataloguing-in-Publication Data
A catalogue record for this book is available from the British Library

Library of Congress Cataloging-in-Publication Data
Names: Shand, Rory, author.
Title: The governance of sustainable rural renewal : a comparative
global perspective / Rory Shand.
Description: Abingdon, Oxon ; New York, NY : Routledge, 2016.
Identifiers: LCCN 2015050295| ISBN 9781138898493 (hardback) |
ISBN 9781315708546 (ebook)
Subjects: LCSH: Rural renewal–Environmental policy. | Rural
renewal–Government policy. | Rural development–Environmental
aspects. | Rural development–Government policy. | Land use, Rural–
Government policy. | Land use, Rural–Environmental aspects.
Classification: LCC HT435 .S43 2016 | DDC 307.1/412–dc23
LC record available at http://lccn.loc.gov/2015050295

ISBN: 978-1-138-89849-3 (hbk)
ISBN: 978-0-8153-6452-8 (pbk)

Typeset in Sabon
by Wearset Ltd, Boldon, Tyne and Wear

Contents

Figures

Tables

Acknowledgements

This book was almost as long in the making as an idea as in terms of writing the text, and as such there are several people to whom I wish to offer my thanks. Both professionally and personally, this work – and its author – owes each of these people heartfelt thanks, and probably, in the case of one or two, should ask for forgiveness for constant requests for feedback and opinions! First, I offer my sincere thanks to the team at Routledge, particularly Senior Editorial Assistant Helen Bell, who is always happy to offer opinions, advice and encouragement. I also want to thank several colleagues and friends. My colleagues, Professor Joyce Liddle (Aix-Marseille), Professor Charles Lees (Bath), Dr Lorraine McCormack (Brunel) and the Public Services group at Manchester Metropolitan University – Frank Carr, Dave McKinney, Dr Annabel Kiernan, Dr Roz Fox and Dr Anthony May – continue to be an inspiration and an example, and never seem to tire of helping me. My friends and family, who make me brave enough to keep dreaming, supported and encouraged me through the writing of this book as they do in everything. Particularly, I want to thank the brilliant and hilarious Alana Hunter, not only for her friendship but also for her unyielding patience, Hannah Brimblecombe, and my oldest friends James Horslen and Dr Michael Roberts. I want to thank my family, especially my parents Margaret and John and my cousin Jenny Fenwick for everything. Most of all, I want to thank Helen, for all her laughter and support and strength day after day. Without her this book would not have been written, and it is to her that it is dedicated.

Rory Shand
Manchester
December 2015

Abbreviations

APM	Asymmetric Power Model
DARD	Department of Agriculture and Rural Development
DBSA	Development Bank of Southern Africa
DIFD	Department of International Development
DPM	Differentiated Polity Model
DRDLR	Department of Rural Development and Land Reform
ECDC	Eastern Cape Development Corporation
ECRDA	Eastern Cape Rural Development Agency
EEC	Endangered Ecological Communities
EU	European Union
FFFR	Foundation for Rural and Regional Renewal
LED	Local Economic Development
ND RDC	North Dakota Rural Development Corporation
NPG	New Public Governance
NPM	New Public Management
RDP	Rural Development Programme
REP	Rural Economic Partnership
RFS	Rural Fire Service
UFH	University of Fort Hare
USDA	United States Development Agency
USDA RD	United States Development Agency Rural Development
VoG	Vale of Glamorgan
WG	Welsh Government

1 Why rural renewal?

Challenges and context for governance

Introduction

Why a book on the governance of rural renewal? First, to address the focus on urban renewal, regeneration and development; second, to capture and examine some of the foremost case studies of rural renewal and its governance, and to compare these case studies cross-nationally; and third, and importantly, to address from a governance perspective the need for greater linkage between urban and rural renewal, in terms of lesson drawing and resource management, i.e. through partnerships, networks, resource management, targets or related government (often, most typically, national level) projects. This book focuses on the key debates and questions around the governance of rural renewal across comparative national case studies, but many of these debates are relevant for urban renewal as well – particularly around resource management and distribution, meeting targets set out in projects and sustainability challenges around food, water, and ecology. Moreover, the patterns of governance design set out in each of the case studies bear resemblance to one another and also to a far broader set of partnership or network arrangements, both in design and delivery. These ideals underpin the design of governance in the case study areas, and several others, as well as in urban renewal settings and contexts. Evidently, these governance arrangements are responses to problems such as resource management or funding, but, equally, these issues cannot and do not exist in splendid isolation. Though several examples of renewal projects in urban contexts have proven to be too ambitious and large in scale – see, for example, the Thames Gateway project (Shand, 2013) – rural renewal programmes are confronted by the same governance issues. These challenges and their wider contexts are set out in the following sections.

Challenges and context

The challenges for rural renewal, then, are centred on the design and implementation of governance. As noted above, these governance delivery mechanisms – such as, most typically, partnerships and networks – are driven by the need to deliver renewal programmes which address a number of key problem areas. For example, rural renewal programmes set out to address a wide range of issues for improvement and cohesion, such as transport, water and food security, education, community engagement and participation and farming.

This book sets out to unite the ideas expounded by scholars concerned with the governance of urban regeneration with examples from rural case studies. The book aims to link the debates around best practice in the governance of regeneration in cities with best examples from rural case studies selected globally. The literature refers to debates around human geography, sustainability and development, or urbanisation, but from a public administration or political science perspective; there is relatively little written about the governance of rural regeneration projects and settings as case studies, neither nationally nor globally, or in a wider comparative context. There is some existing literature which compares across two nations, but virtually none with a wider cross-national comparative approach. There is also a lack of linkage between the academic debates and the practice agenda in this area, which this book seeks to address by dedicated sections in each chapter summarising both the relevant linkages between academic debate and practice, as well as a dedicated chapter on the relationship between theory and practice in the area of rural renewal.

The rationale for the book is to examine a range of case study examples of rural regeneration projects through the public administration lens, focusing on how governance arrangements in rural settings work. A key focus of the book will be the roles of communities, business and tiers of governance (local, regional, national and supra national) in terms of delivery and funding. By drawing on a range of global case studies, the book aims to identify best practice in governance, applicable to both academic conceptual debates and to practitioners engaged in the real-world governance of regeneration. While there are substantial political science, sociology and geography debates within the existing academic literature around food security, fair trade, urban–rural divides and supply chains, there is little on the way that governance in comparative global case study settings operates in achieving or underpinning rural renewal programmes.

Though existing literature in the governance and politics field (and related areas such as human geography) addresses some of these points in terms of rural renewal, there is no real national-level comparison across countries. While there is some highly detailed and excellent work at the national and sub-national level on the topic (Osborne *et al.*, 2002, 2004; Long and Woods, 2011) and some comparative analysis at the national level from a governance perspective, this is not comparative in a global sense. Therefore, this book sets out to build on and contribute to the debates fostered by the existing literature in academic circles and in practice, but also seeks to build on this in two main ways: first, by broadening existing academic and practice debates on the governance of rural renewal to a cross-national comparative level, focused on communities, governments and businesses; and, second, by linking these debates in more depth to the much larger existing body of work on the governance of urban renewal. These key themes are underpinned by the theoretical approach of policy networks, drawing particularly on the notion of interpretivism put forward by Bevir (2004) and Bevir and Rhodes (2006; 2011), of which there is much deeper and more detailed discussion in the subsequent chapter. The key themes are examined in each of the case study areas, in Chapters 4–7 and are applied in both comparative and praxis – theory and practice – contexts. The following sections discuss each chapter in more detail.

Chapter synopsis

1   Why rural renewal? Challenges and context for governance
    This chapter sets the context for the key debates and questions which concern the book in rural renewal initiatives globally, drawn both from the academic literatures and from the grey practice literature. This chapter examines the role of governance mechanisms and projects in a broad global context, before focusing on each of the national-level case studies.
2   The urban–rural divide? Debates on rural renewal in theory and practice
    This chapter summarises the academic literatures and the grey literatures, focusing on renewal and governance. The existing academic debates around the role of communities, governance mechanisms and local-regional rural renewal initiatives are examined, and contrasted with local, regional and national discussions of urban renewal. The chapter then moves on to summarise the relevant, historical and recent debates around governance as a framework or method from both academic and practice sources.
3   Comparing rural renewal: Examining themes, actors and outcomes
    This chapter examines and applies the key governance approaches and models to the case study areas, setting up a governance model which draws upon the frameworks of New Public Management and New Public Governance, and which can be applied and tested to the empirical national case study chapters. This represents one of the key contributions of the book, advancing the academic literature and the conceptual approaches of governance, each linked to practice.
4   UK: Vale of Glamorgan
    This chapter examines the Vale of Glamorgan rural renewal initiative, focusing on the role of communities in governance, agriculture and business, linked to conceptual and topical debates for both theory and practice, such as targets, progress and outcomes of projects, and co-production.

Theory and practice

This book will be of interest to both academic and practitioner markets.
While not a dedicated textbook, it would be a suitable and topical teaching
resource for undergraduate, taught postgraduate and research students, as
well as for scholars engaged in similar and related fields of study. The use
of dedicated specific sections in each of the chapters – in particular, the
case study sections drawing on national-level empirical cases – links
research to teaching, and research to practice. This book would be a relevant resource for practitioners across the field such as NGOs, local and
national levels of governments, planners, architects, farmers, community
projects and small, medium and large businesses. The case studies are
based on ongoing programmes and goals, which are purposefully anchored
within the broader context of rural renewal. The case studies, therefore,

have implications for broader rural renewal concerns in other national case study settings, such as: policy design and delivery; scope of the project and its funding; relations between partnerships or networks of actors engaged in delivery of the project; resource management and sustainability (transportation, supply chains, food and water) and ecology. The applied nature of the case studies in this book is therefore aimed at gathering findings which examine and map the governance process in terms of design and delivery. The theoretical focus of this (set out in more depth in the following section) is concerned with examining the relations between actors in governance and drawing upon relevant policy networks frameworks to evaluate the progress of projects in the case study areas in terms of the effectiveness of governance – that is, the management of resources and whether targets are met. Evidently, these aspects of governance – meeting the project's aims, managing budgets and resources, and ensuring effective co-operation and communication between actors – are not just theoretical concerns. These are key aspects of effective project governance for practitioners at several levels and from varying sectors. These actors, in the case study areas but also in terms of lesson drawing into other case studies of governing rural renewal, are drawn from the public services, from local and central government, from government created agencies, the voluntary sector and the private sector. The preponderance of networks and partnerships in urban renewal projects in large cities or other urban mega-regions, and the wider focus in governance and public management on partnership or network delivery (set out in the following chapter in more depth), is also represented in rural renewal settings. In order to examine and evaluate these governance mechanisms, the policy networks approach is adopted.

Approach and methodology

This research adopts the policy networks approach in underpinning key themes and literature debates, across both theory and practice. The policy networks approach provides (as is discussed in Chapters 2 and 3 in more detail) a theory, framework or method with which to evaluate and examine the partnerships and networks engaged in delivery in the case study areas. These governance arrangements are subject to issues such as communication, funding, co-ordination and power. Within the notion of power in and across the governance design in each of the case studies, policy networks focuses on relations within the network, distribution and (in)equalities of power, and the constructions and interpretations of individual roles by the actors in the network. This research draws upon the approach of Bevir, and Bevir and Rhodes, to examine the interaction between these actors in the network in terms of project design, delivery, power relations and interpretation of roles. This approach is set out in more detail in the subsequent literature review chapter and the methodology chapter, and then applied to the case studies and discussion.

Comparing across cases studies

As set out above, the four case studies come from differing national contexts both in terms of institutional design and of governance design. Additionally, the case studies are couched in the context of different histories,
rituals and constructions of meanings around tradition, nationhood and
politics. These are difficult to compare, even in a most different or most
similar systems design context, as the role of meanings is highly important
for communities; in each of the case study areas, the engagement and participation of communities in the governance and delivery of the rural
renewal programmes is a desired target. However, the cases represent different geographic areas, each with their own history and identity in terms
of politics, communities and (resultant) governance. The cases, therefore,
represent a comparison across differing global examples. Previous work in
this field tends to focus on more regional or national cases, or a focus by
some scholars on communities (as will be discussed at length in the following chapter). In contrast to debates in the academic literature on urban
renewal programmes, there is little comparison at the national level, from
a governance perspective. Key thinkers and debates in the field of rural
renewal have focused on principles of management or delivery, but not to
a great extent in comparing across national case studies using governance
frameworks and approaches. There is some excellent work in terms of
communities and local focus (Gallent and Robinson, 2012) and also in
terms of public management and policy making. This book differs from
the above (and from those concerned with urban renewal) by offering a
cross-national comparative focus, rather than a single country focus or a
local, regional or national focus anchored in a single national case study.
Additionally, the book seeks to further interdisciplinary study and linkages
between these areas. The book sets out to compare across the four different cases, and then goes on to draw broader conclusions around further
cases and the implications of the findings in the four cases of the UK, the
USA, Australia and South Africa, both for governance actors engaged in
rural renewal programmes in practice, and for the theoretical implications
of applying the policy networks approach to cross-national case studies of
rural renewal and its governance. The cases, and the related grey literature
produced by the actors charged with delivery within them, are discussed in
more depth in Chapter 3. The book, though anchored in governance literature and these key debates, as well as adopting as a conceptual framework the policy networks approach, stresses inter-disciplinarity. Of course,
in practice, rural renewal projects do not recognise disciplinary boundaries.
The key themes of the book, drawn out in each of the case study areas,
reflect this.

2 The urban–rural divide?

Debates on rural renewal in theory and practice

The first sections of this literature review focused chapter will build on the key themes and cases set out in the introductory chapter by placing the debates around rural renewal in the case studies in the broader governance context of the literature, initially focusing on unpacking the theoretical approaches and key discussions, before in the latter sections of the chapter then moving on to the more practice-focused grey literature, produced by the range of key actors engaged in the delivery of the projects across the four rural renewal case study areas. The initial sections will deal with the literature around governance and renewal – in some aspects rural, in some urban. The chapter will then move on to discuss the main relevant governance frameworks and theoretical approaches, reviewing the governance literature, before moving on to a more specific discussion of the grey literature produced in the case study areas, which will be examined in this chapter and then expanded upon and applied in the four rural case study areas in Chapters 4 to 7. First, however, it is necessary to examine the key literatures and debates relating to the governance of renewal programmes, and in beginning to examine these debates, the role of terminology is increasingly important.

This book refers to rural *renewal* and regeneration programmes across four very distinct and varying areas (discussed in more depth in the institutional and comparative governance sections of the following chapter). The emphasis is on renewal because there is complexity around the meanings of terms such as regeneration or development. To be sure, the four rural renewal programmes examined in this book could equally be referred to as regeneration programmes, but, in some areas, this term has lost emphasis or meaning (for example, the term regeneration has little meaning in the French context). Moreover, despite being en vogue in a number of cases 10 years ago, for example, the focus on large-scale regeneration has become far more focused on business development and house building since the global financial crisis and, though these are important elements of both urban and rural initiatives, they are not holistic measures, alongside community engagement and management (Liddle and Diamond, 2007), the development of public infrastructure, and the integration of sustainable and ecological measures. In addition, the long term and complex aims of both rural and urban renewal – or regeneration – initiatives have not achieved many of their longer-term aims or legacies. The discussion of what happens to ideas of renewal now, or in the aftermath of large-scale renewal projects given the focus on the localism agenda in the UK, the role of the media and the era of austerity, is captured in the excellent *After Urban Regeneration* (Matthews and O'Brien, 2015).

Governing rural renewal

There are also a number of other rural renewal cases that this book does not focus upon. However, these are each noteworthy for their shared themes with the rural renewal programmes examined in this research. These typically tend to be the development of areas such as tourism and agriculture in rural areas or regions. There is also emphasis in terms of developing civic capacity and public infrastructure, but the overarching theme of these (many) rural renewal initiatives is the focus on community participation in the governance of the programme. This is also true of urban renewal programmes, but this tends to be one of many complex aims in the urban context; the focus on community participation in governance of rural renewal is perhaps one of sharper focus because in order to be successful, the community needs to buy in to the renewal programme to maximise the chances of success and sustainable outcomes.

Moreover, from a governance perspective (and given the predilection for partnership or network approaches to governing these renewal programmes) the community in rural areas is often embedded in smaller more entrenched networks, encompassing businesses, civic organisations and public services. For example, the role of schools is an important hub for rural renewal in areas of Canada. The role of schools in Nova Scotia as a mechanism for community engagement and participation is drawn upon in turning small schools into community hubs (Bennett *et al.*, 2013). This approach sees the role of an existing community facility used to build a focal point – a hub – to provide a platform for community engagement in areas such as development, becoming more sustainable and in acting as a pathway to rural renewal for the community. Elsewhere, the role of the partnership approach to governance is also prominent in design, delivery and the aims of rural renewal: for example, this approach is present in the key themes of rural renewal programmes in cases as diverse as Northern Ireland and in Japan. In the Northern Irish case, the rural renewal programme is driven by the Department of Agriculture and Rural Development (DARD). DARD is charged with delivering the 2014–2020 Rural Development Programme (DRP) in Northern Ireland. This programme is funded by the Europe 2020 strategy and, as a result, the DARD has to comply with the funding conditions from the EU level in their design and delivery of the rural renewal programme. The DRP in Northern Ireland has focused on the inclusion of the key themes and requirements from the supra national level and has reflected the six priorities of the EU funding in the governance structure nationally, to encompass: knowledge transfer; farm competitiveness and risk management; food chain organisation; restoring and enhancing ecosystems; promoting resource efficiency; and social inclusion, poverty reduction and rural economic development. The DARD has included six sub-groups in the governance structure in the delivery of rural renewal to reflect these key areas. In addition, the Europe 2020 funding includes the requirement to set up a Programme Development Stakeholder Consultation Group. This facet of the governance of rural renewal emphasises the linkage between the supra national, national, local levels and the community – however, it should be noted that the funding also highlights the need to work with existing partners and stakeholders, emphasising the partnership approach to the rural renewal programmes' governance structure. The consultation group in Northern Ireland was established in 2012 and its function is one of an advisory nature though it also reflects the partnership governance focus in its makeup:

> This group acts as an advisory body. The Group includes a wide range of stakeholders, including the farming unions, environmental NGOs, local government, local action groups, universities, business groups and representatives from the rural social economy.
> (www.dardni.gov.uk/index/rural-development-programme, 2015)

The role of supra national funding and the partnership arrangements, roles and power relations between these large funding actors will be discussed in more depth in the Vale of Glamorgan case study in Chapter 4. These themes of partnership, agriculture and business development are reflected in a Japanese rural renewal example, where the focus on agriculture, population growth, community participation and economic developments are underpinning themes and aims (Odagiri, 2008: 12). The role of population is also key to the design and delivery of governance in rural renewal. Increasing population, ageing communities and talent leaving are all aspects of migration that have implications for the governance and success or failure of rural renewal initiatives, with the role of migration a central cause in the need for rural renewal programmes (Stockdale, 2006).

As noted in the previous, introductory chapter, though there are some excellent existing debates in the literature around governance and related areas, there is no real national-level comparison across countries. While there is some highly detailed and excellent work at the national and sub-national level on the topic (Osborne *et al.*, 2002, 2004; Long and Woods, 2011) and some comparative analysis at the national level from a governance perspective, this is not comparative in a global sense. In terms of these national-, sub-national- and community-focused studies, there is great scholarly coverage of rural renewal and regeneration in community settings, locally, regionally and nationally. This book sets out to unite the ideas expounded by scholars concerned with the governance of renewal with examples from the UK that demonstrate the role of the voluntary sector in the governance of renewal. The literature refers to debates around human geography, sustainability and renewal, or urbanisation but, from a public administration or political science perspective, there is relatively little written about the role of collaborative governance in rural renewal projects and settings as case studies, certainly nationally, or in a comparative context. There is also a lack of linkage between the academic debates and the practice agenda in this area, which the book seeks to address by dedicated sections in each case study chapter summarising both the relevant linkages between academic debate and practice, as well as a more detailed discussion of the theory-practice relationship in Chapter 8.

Governance of renewal

A key focus of the rural renewal cases is the role of the voluntary sector working with communities, business and tiers of governance (local, regional, national, and supra national) in terms of delivery and funding, aiming to identify best practice in governance, applicable to both academic conceptual debates and to practitioners engaged in the real-world governance of renewal. While there are substantial political science, sociology and geography debates within the existing academic literature around food security, fair trade, urban–rural divides and supply chains, there is little on the way that governance in comparative case study settings operates in working with the voluntary sector in renewal programmes. This book seeks to contribute to the research in this area of debate (Alcock, 2011) and on the voluntary sector from a governance perspective more broadly both in terms of national, comparative and European focus on third sector and governance, working with the public services and local and regional tiers, both in terms of networks, partnerships and New Public Governance and related issues of co-production of services and governance delivery. Rural (and urban) renewal programmes have also drawn the voluntary sector and governance into collaboration.

This chapter examines and applies the key governance debates and practices in rural renewal and in partnership delivery, to the case study areas, setting up a governance model which draws upon the frameworks of interpretivism (Bevir, 2004, 2009, 2010; Bevir and Rhodes, 2003, 2006, 2008, 2011; Sullivan, 2011; Sorensen, 2002, 2013) and using New Public Governance (Osborne *et al.*, 2004; Osborne, 2006, 2010), and can be applied and tested in renewal programmes at local, regional or national level. In this way, the project advances the academic literature and the conceptual approaches of governance, each linked to practice. The relationship between these actors is examined drawing upon the interpretivist approach.

These organisations have undertaken renewal projects, been responsible for community engagement within them and have set targets and funding levels, linked to renewal initiatives and can be applied and tested to the empirical national case study chapters. This represents one of the key contributions of the book, advancing the academic literature and the conceptual approaches of governance, arguing that communities, private sector teams and organisations have undertaken renewal projects, been responsible for community engagement within them and have set targets and funding levels, linked to renewal initiatives and other community based programmes.

The notion of policy learning and policy transfer in rural renewal

In this chapter and elsewhere in this book, the dominance of partnership or network governance approaches to rural (and urban) renewal programmes is discussed. To be sure, there are some worthy examples of success and sustainability in these initiatives, such as aspects of housing and job creation in Salford Quays in Manchester, Liverpool and Newcastle, and areas of East London in the UK, and in Berlin in Germany, large-scale renewal programmes, and these have been emulated across supra national, national and local renewal contexts which have employed the partnership or network approach in governance. Does this widespread use of the partnership approach in the governance of renewal lead to a type of policy transfer?

The idea of practice in one nation state emulating practice in another is drawn from political science (see for example Rose, 1991; Dolowitz and Marsh 1996). There are a number of broadly synonymous terms for this, including lesson drawing, emulation, harmonisation and policy transfer, although Dolowitz and Marsh (1996) argue that policy transfer is the most useful term since, with the possible exception of harmonisation, others mentioned above imply that the process is essentially voluntary, whereas this might not always be the case. For our purposes here, policy transfer refers to a process where:

> Knowledge about policies, administrative arrangements, institutions, etc. in one time and/or place is used in the development of policies, administrative arrangements and institutions in another time and/or place.
>
> (Dolowitz and Marsh, 1996: 344)

It can be argued that the notion of policy transfer offers a novel theoretical perspective on how renewal policies and practices, in this case related to rural renewal, are transferred from one state to another in the context of partnership delivery. This is based on an examination of the literature on policy transfer to show *what* is transferred, *who* is engaged in policy transfer, *types* of policy transfer (voluntary and coercive) and factors affecting its success or failure. In considering *what* is transferred, the literature focuses on elements of policy that are closely mirrored in aspects of governance strategies. These might range from the less tangible such as ideas for policy, attitudes and even ideological rhetoric, through to specific goals, programme structures, policy content and detailed techniques of implementation (see, for example, Wolman, 1992; Dolowitz and Marsh, 1996). These categories could equally apply to the goals, content and implementation of rural renewal; Second, a range of actors can be shown to be involved in policy transfer, including civil servants, politicians, political parties, policy experts and supra national organisations such as the World Trade Organisation (WTO) or the European Union (EU). However, given the power and geographical scope of many key actors engaged in the governance and delivery of renewal programmes, it would be surprising if they, too, did not play a role in the transfer of policies between states. Third, it is possible to broadly categorise policy transfer as either voluntary or coercive (Dolowiz and Marsh, 1996). Voluntary transfer is said by many authors to be driven by dissatisfaction with the status quo (see, for example, Rose, 1991) where current policies are failing in some sense. Of course, the perception of failure is not uncontested territory. For example, Dolowitz and Marsh (1996) point out that whether high unemployment or high inflation is the better indicator of policy failure depends largely on the political perspective being adopted. In any event, the notion of dissatisfaction implies a 'demand' driving policy transfer rather than it being pushed from the 'supply' side. For this the discussion now turns to coercive transfer.

Coercive transfer describes, for example, how one government might force another to adopt certain policies, although Dolowitz and Marsh (1996) argue that this very direct coercion is rare. More commonly, institutions such as the WTO or the International Monetary Fund (IMF) place financial pressures on states to adopt, for example, deregulation. Finally, the failure of policy transfer has been related to three factors, namely: uninformed transfer; incomplete transfer; and inappropriate transfer (Dolowitz and Marsh, 2000). We should also remind ourselves that policy transfer is occurring in the context of globalisation, argued by some to bring decreasing state influence on economic decisions and policies more generally. For example, referring to a range of policy areas such as finance, crime and health, Woods claims that 'Policy makers worry that they are losing yet more of their control over their own economies and policy choices, as key policy instruments seem to dangle just out of reach' (2002: 25). Furthermore, 'Globalization has also affected domestic politics and thereby the capacity of governments to manage these new forces' (Woods, 2000: 26). Policies on many aspects of economic activity are therefore de-territorialised. This in turn means governments have less control.

In understanding a possible transfer of policy, or barriers to this, the notion of coercive policy transfer (Dolowitz and Marsh, 1996) can be drawn upon. However, ethical dilemmas may occur for actors in governance at the operational level in the rural renewal programmes if lesson drawing (Rose, 1991, 1993), the first stage of policy transfer, has not taken place at a strategic level. If the actor's awareness of cultural norms or existing traditions in a territory is lacking, this is likely to frustrate voluntary implementation of transfer. This, in turn, can lead to certain conditionality in policy transfer, with certain aspects of transfer successful and others not. The partial success of policy transfer can lead to direct imposition or coercive policy transfer: in the case of the transfer of policies, partial success of implementing policy (that is, successful transfer across branches of governance, but unsuccessful lesson drawing of existing norms) may lead to just such an example of coercive unsuccessful policy transfer. This occurrence has also been described by James and Lodge (2003: 189) in critiquing the Dolowitz and Marsh conception of incomplete or inappropriate transfer, as this fails to 'explain policy failure in terms of the process of "transfer" but re-describes the "failure" as a form of "incomplete transfer"' (James and Lodge, 2003: 189). Similarly, Stone (2000) focuses upon the success and failures of NGOs in performing policy transfer, which are subject to the same institutional and cultural constraints and designs in their roles.

The idea of policy learning or policy transfer involves the implicit notion that governance actors seek to have global level policies, regulations and mission statements, but are hampered in these attempts by national context; or, in the rural renewal context, by the nature of differing funding, value systems and norms across nation states. However, turning back to the framework, this is an example of incomplete and inappropriate policy transfer, or specifically as Dolowitz and Marsh (2000) initially suggested, a type of transfer of failure based on an incomplete understanding of the values of the recipient of the transfer. We can see the fallibility of coercion in enacting one set of ethics or mistakenly believing universalist principles will be effective across all nation states. This tells us that policy transfer between the actors may result in confusion rather than cohesion; and that transfer of renewal policy lays bare an incomplete understanding of the informal societal codes which influence behaviours and decisions in the design and delivery of these programmes. We can also note that the appliance of governance partnership or network approaches to rural (and urban) renewal is often despite rather than because of norms and values, and is driven by the wide ranging acceptance of the joined-up or collaborative approach to governance, as the partnership and network approach has been one widely applied in several case study areas in policy realms such as criminal justice, health, and education, as well as renewal and economic development.

The book also draws upon Sorensen's (2013) concepts of political storytelling – meta-governance and governance networks as barriers to democracy and participatory governance – and how this relates to the stories told by leaders to implement and disseminate discourses of trust. As Sorensen suggests, developments in governance, such as the focus on networks in policy design and delivery, increasingly distance people from decision making and increase the layers and separation from governments. This results in several tiers and layers of governance: the government of government, meta-government (and meta-management), largely impenetrable to the public (Sorensen, 2013). Drawing on Sorensen's notion of storytelling by political leaders, storytelling of trust occurs when discourse constructs a linkage between elites and scandal. The subsequent storytelling across society has embedded the idea that politicians and other elites are untrustworthy. The political storytelling then develops as political and financial elites talk about trust and related terms in an effort to reclaim these ideas and present themselves as critical of untrustworthy individuals and practices – such as political elites being perceived as engaged in malpractice engendering mistrust, or the state signing off on the financial bailouts of elites. This leads to a discourse which is constructed on the basis of the public having nobody to trust. This mistrust has been initiated and fostered by events like the financial crisis of 2008 and scandals around MP's expenses. Sorensen suggests that the storytelling process is part of an interactive leadership which engages actors in governance, though he also notes that the complexity of roles and delivery in governance partnerships and networks can frustrate accountability and visibility, both of which are crucial in achieving the outcomes and aims of large-scale rural renewal programmes.

The three broad categories of literature around renewal, development and rural regeneration and renewal in the cases are first, the substantive theoretical debates around networks, partnerships and governance; second, funding and delivery aspects of rural renewal and sustainable development; and, third, the grey literature produced by the range of organisations and actors engaged in the four rural renewal cases. The chapter will focus on notions of interpretive governance debates in relation to the renewal case studies and the role of interpretation in governance partnerships and networks. In the case study areas, the book will focus on the policy networks approach and this approach will be employed as a framework to examine the construction of roles, inequalities and power relations across the governance partnerships in the cases. In applying the policy networks approach, the book focuses on the influence of resource allocation, role construction and power relations on the rules of the game in governance in each case study area.

The governance debates, and the focus on networks and governance arising from the use of multi-agency and New Public Governance approaches, have driven behavioural debates within the policy networks approach. This focus on constructivist meanings and interpretivism has centred upon how actors are affected by the ways in which they interpret their own roles and that of others in governance partnerships or collaborations. This book accepts Bevir's (2004, 2009) and Bevir and Rhodes' (2003, 2008, 2011) focus on the interpretivist nature of the DPM, an assertion later challenged by scholars advancing the APM in terms of power relations and role interpretation in constructivism and critical realism (Marsh, 2011).

In applying interpretive governance in governance partnerships, and in following studies such as Sullivan's (2011) performing governance, Sorensen's (2002, 2013) political storytelling and Gains' (2003) work on roles in governance agencies, the importance of roles are indeed constructed by those who occupy them and in response to the ways others perceive these roles, and, in that stance, we then advance the argument that these roles are further constructed by the roles of governance – the echoes of previous performers in these roles, and their respective parts.

Governance partnerships are also subject to the interpretations of actors and the construction of roles in terms of the histories and influences of the individual actors engaged in governance. These influences may act as constraints or opportunities, given the differing histories that actors have experienced. The governance agency, for example, may have been set up specifically to fund and deliver projects. Drawing on Bevir, these pressures drive the interpretations and constructions individuals have of their own and others' roles. There is much debate in recent governance literature around the apparent demise of NPM, or rather, its enduring nature. If anything, when examining practice and the scholarly debates, the tenacity of NPM and also, and more latterly, the role of multi-agency working are striking.

This complexity and hyperactivity (Catney *et al.*, 2000) in governance has led to the formation of several agencies and an emphasis on partnerships or networks in the delivery of governance projects and in public service management. Whilst the literature has focused on these kinds of partnership and network delivery and the roles and relations between the constituent actors in governance, the focus in this book is one that examines the delivery of collaborative governance, characterised by partnerships, 'networks', multi-agency settings or New Public Governance (Osborne, 2010). Through New Public Governance, the role of partnerships and networks has been brought into a more practical focus; in following Bevir and Rhodes (and many other notable contributions such as Kjaer) the book follows the notion that power relations in these governance mechanisms are affected by role construction. But in developing this argument further, we suggest that policy decisions and policy outcomes are directly affected by the roles of governance: the ways that individuals' interpret and then subsequently carry out theirs and others' respective roles.

Therefore, in examining roles and relations in partnerships and networks, the ideas of interpretation and recognition (of size, history, function, etc.) are highly relevant to practice situations such as the rural renewal programmes across the cases. Gains and Stoker (2011) discuss the concept of leadership roles and the relations between them with regard to local governance, while Sullivan (2011) sets out the idea of performing governance. This book draws upon each of these concepts, their roles in governance and the power relations and structures they create in delivery. It also examines how these constrain the constituent partners in terms of their own role, how they interpret this role, and what these constraining factors are in terms of aspects of delivery such as budget, size and proximity to government.

In terms of partnership governance and delivery, employing policy networks allows us to examine the ways inequalities, power relations and delivery in the partnership construct the roles of actors and the resultant mode of delivery. For example, if the community actors (Osborne *et al.*, 2004) are engaged in the process in terms of design, this enables them to construct their role in a positive manner which will then have implications for their construction of other actors roles in the partnership or policy network, taking into account the importance of the weight of budgetary awarding power, decision making and the role of national, federal or local levels as established governance actors and the creation of agencies to manage and coordinate large-scale renewal programmes (in common with several other aspects of partnership or network governance which involve steering or coordination by agencies).

This leads us to examine the function of roles as power, because roles create advantages enjoyed by a partner in governance who understands the symbolism of rituals and the previous incumbents of their own role. These power relations create – or some would suggest, perpetuate – advantages to those who understand their own role in terms of roles. Drawing on the Bevir and Rhodes concept of 'power and resistance' (Davies, 2005) the power relations between roles, and the influence these have, there are asymmetries between the roles which are impossible to ignore for these who occupy the roles. The following sections examine the role of asymmetries in power relations between the roles:

> Drawing upon the policy networks tradition to examine the roles of actors in delivering these roles within governance, we can identify relations of power between the roles. Notions of pluralism and neo-pluralism, of asymmetries and disaggregation of power (Gains, 2003), are examined in this essay as the products of roles, echoes and role construction, which reinforce relations between actors in governance. However, we are not intending to focus on the key debates around power relations between actors in governance networks here (inter alia, Borzel, 1998, 2003; Dowding, 1995, 2001). Therefore, agents interpret their role and that of others and this has an effect on actors' behaviour in the policy process, and the 'structures that constrain and

facilitate agents' (Marsh, 2008: 737). Therefore, while Bevir and Rhodes suggest that the focus on power relations reifies the role of the centre and privileges institutional constraints, their narrative emphasises the actions and beliefs of actors through their conception of their role in the policy process.

(Shand, 2013: 8–9)

The interpretivist framework is grounded in the notion of roles and meanings. In governance settings, these are often highlighted in the design and delivery of projects (in these cases, rural renewal programmes). The extent of governance networks and partnerships is highly prevalent in policies, or in the delivery of local and national public service provision. The process of interpretivism in governance – crucially, the construction and interpretation of roles in these partnership and network arrangements – is central to how the constituent partners view themselves, each other and their respective roles in delivery. First, the actor A has their own construction and interpretation of their role in governance, design and delivery. Actor B likewise, and so on, across each actor in governance. These actors' own views of their roles are then influenced by the other actors' interpretations, and they contribute to the meanings and internalisation of the role. As Mead (1955) suggests in *Mind, Self and Society*, the way we see ourselves is influenced by others' reactions to us. This is, if anything, a process which is heightened under the structure of governance arrangements such as partnerships or networks, where there are several different roles involved in delivery, each with its own history, shadows and expectations. The focus on roles and power relations between actors in governance partnerships in renewal is not one which is constrained to rural renewal. In my previous research on the governance of large-scale *urban* renewal programmes, the importance of roles and relations across governance delivery was a vital element (Shand, 2013) of success or failure in the outcomes of the renewal programmes.

Bevir and Rhodes suggest that these discussions of power relations reify the role of the centre and overstate the influence of institutional constraints, suggesting it is the actions and beliefs of actors which shape relations through their conception of their role in the policy process. As noted earlier in this chapter, the notion of roles and echoes is present in studies such as Gains and Stoker's (2011) research on local leadership. The echoes of these roles resound in roles, titles and functions. Though function is routinely (and wrongly) confused and conflated with power, the effects of roles and echoes of power are important and pervasive even at micro levels. If we turn to the notion of associational man, this is not a term which reflects a positive difference, but one which emphasises the importance of roles. In terms of relating and locating the book in debates on the role of the voluntary sector more generally in public provision of services, this book draws upon work such as the third sector in Europe (Osborne,

2010) and the role of non-profits and the voluntary sector in governance arrangements and delivery (Osborne, 2011) Though existing literature in the governance and politics field (and related areas such as Human Geography) addresses some of these points in terms of the governance of development, there is limited national-level comparison across countries which focus on the role of development and the voluntary sector in governance. While there is some highly detailed and excellent work at the national and sub-national level on the topic (Edwards *et al.*, 2000; Osborne *et al.*, 2004) the book seeks to contribute to the research in this area of debate (Alcock, 2011) and on the voluntary sector from a governance perspective more broadly both in terms of national, comparative and European focus on third sector and governance, working with the public services and local and national tiers, both in terms of networks, partnerships and New Public Governance and related issues of co-production of services and governance delivery. The book also draws on the scholarly work in the area of the voluntary sector and governance. Therefore, the book sets out to build on and contribute to the debates fostered by the existing literature in academic circles and in practice, but also seeks to build on this in two main ways: first, by broadening existing academic and practice debates on the governance of development to a cross-national comparative level, focused on communities, governments and businesses; and, second, to link these debates in more depth to the much larger existing body of work on governance of urban development.

Case study areas: rural renewal and governance

The following sections examine the key themes and debates across the practice literature in the case study areas; that is, the debates and key themes within the literature produced by the organisations engaged in delivery. This grey literature, traditionally, set out the key competencies and roles of the delivery agencies and their partners in the project, as well as the key targets and performance indicators the project was aiming to achieve (such as, more sustainable use of farmland, more community engagement, more business integration, etc.). The following sections examine such debates in the context of each of the four case study areas, beginning with the Vale of Glamorgan programme in the UK.

UK: Vale of Glamorgan

The key themes of the Vale of Glamorgan programme are set around, to a degree, both urban and rural renewal, as there is a focus within the project on the town centre in Barry. However, the Vale of Glamorgan programme also focuses on the renewal of rural areas, and can be seen as one of the most innovative types of rural renewal initiative, certainly in the UK. The key actors in the programme have produced several pieces which underpin the project and the role creation and construction of these key actors. For example, in the *Local Development Strategic Plan for Rural Communities*, the main actors in the partnership are set out, and the key targets of the programmes evaluated. The drivers behind the renewal initiative are much like those found in any rural (or indeed urban) renewal programme, such as employment statistics in the renewal area, and the age of the population (www.valeofglamorgan.gov.uk/Documents/Working/Regeneration/Final% 20LDS%20REVISED%20OCT09%20_2_.pdf). This publication goes on to discuss the context and background for the need for rural renewal; driven by economic factors such as the national (and global) economic downtown and the resultant austerity measures. The *Local Development Strategic for Rural Communities* is a wide ranging document, which reflects the aims of the rural renewal programme in the Vale. The employment statistics in the area and business integration are discussed at some length, which reflects again the key aims and themes of the programme. The strategy also focuses on the accessibility of the rural community to services – both in terms of public services and the related transport links. The key partners in the pro-gramme are drawn from the public, private and voluntary sectors, and have much in common with several other renewal initiatives. The partners are drawn from a cross-sectoral range, and are setting out to work in part-nership in terms of strategy and delivery of the rural renewal programme. These organisations are representative of several rural actors, but also focused to a large degree on the role of the voluntary sector in the area, together with strong representation from the local farming community. This could perhaps demonstrate the existence of networks in the area driving the projects, which the empirical research will investigate. The range of actors engaged in this initiative demonstrates the partnership or network approach, which is widely used in several renewal, regeneration or development (in common with many other policy project areas). This approach differs in some ways from a multi-agency approach – we see a range of actors represented in the design of the initiative – but we also see the region represented in the type of actors, clustered around the local, agricultural and voluntary sectors, working with young people's groups, local and town level councils, and small businesses in the area; there is a good deal of commonality in terms of remit. This case study represents a very large number of actors engaged in the design and delivery of the rural renewal initiative, emphasising coordination in delivery, which will be examined in the empirical chapter drawing upon the policy networks and interpretivist approach. The Vale of Glamorgan renewal initiative has several small key areas, linked to broader policy priorities of anti-poverty, social inclusion, education and health. Within each of these key priority goals are set renewal projects based around improving town centres, flora and fauna, and educational opportunities. Though a large number of part-ners and actors are engaged in the design and delivery of this renewal pro-gramme, there are several smaller key themes; in terms of governance, this mirrors the design of the programme through the delivery of targeted, smaller project and area specific goals.

Australia: New South Wales

The Australian NSW rural renewal case study focuses, again, upon the role of partnership in design and delivery in governance. At the national level, the main driver for rural renewal projects, and evidently within that their governance, is the Department of Infrastructure and Regional Development, and related to but not within this level, the Foundation for Rural and Regional Renewal (FRRR). The FRRR, since its inception, has funded projects worth $25 million. The FRRR is not part of the Department of Infrastructure and Regional Development, but rather a charitable foundation (as opposed, say, to a government agency as we see in several other rural- and urban-renewal programmes). In the NSW area alone, the FRRR supports dozens of projects, and this territory is just one such example of national support across the whole of Australia for rural renewal. The Department of Infrastructure and Regional Development and the FRRR are central nationally and across NSW. The FRRR has produced several publications, notably the *Evaluation of Performance Over the First Ten Years and the Contribution the FRRR Makes to Rural and Regional Australia* (2010), an evaluation report which focuses on the grant successes in projects supported by the FRRR; an analysis of the number of applications, both successful and unsuccessful; and an overview of feedback from the projects the FRRR has supported. The evaluation report focuses in the main on the record of the FRRR, but does not address the role of governance to any great extent. However, the FRRR does emphasise the role of partnership working in its success in supporting rural renewal programmes, and indeed the need to extend the partnership model of delivery in rural renewal. The strategy notes the need for:

> Deepening the partnership model and extending to new partnerships.... It is recommended that FRRR extend its proposition where this evaluation has indicated demand. This includes a stronger interstate presence, increased use of technology and expanding the scope of services. The key priorities for the FRRR to extend its operations are to build on existing relationships and to strategically develop new relationships. This includes sharing.
>
> (FRRR, 2010: 6)

The FRRR has also produced periodic reviews of its educational programmes. Not only do these give an evaluation and an overview of key metrics, such as targets in projects, they also set up the importance of education within and across rural renewal and its governance in NSW and Australia as a whole.

FRRR began in 2000, setting up its permanent headquarters, appropriately in the home of Sidney Myer's first store – in the regional Victorian city of Bendigo. There it continues to operate from historic Dudley House and to follow the principles and ideals first set down by the Regional Australia Summit. To date, FRRR has allocated $12.3 million and has leveraged millions to help communities renew themselves.

(FRRR, 2010)

South Africa: Eastern Cape

This case study is driven by the Eastern Cape Rural Development Agency (ECRDA). The programmes and projects the ECRDA coordinates and delivers are focused on objectives which emphasise the role of communities in terms of participation and delivery of the rural renewal initiative. The aims set out below also foreground the role of actors from different sectors, linking public and private sector actors with community groups; and also focusing these cooperative aspects linked to the design, delivery and funding of the rural renewal programme:

- Address obstacles to progress forestry development – such as licensing, land-use planning, community structures, private sector involvement, stakeholder participation, resource availability.
- Provide support to communities involved in forestry development: facilitation of suitable partnership arrangements with companies, enabling structures to govern with responsibility, oversight to projects.
- Ensure that administration and accounting of funds is at the required standards.
- Plan and package projects to enable implementation.

(www.ecrda.co.za/Forestry.html, accessed 29/6/15)

The area in the Eastern Cape, in common with other rural renewal initiatives across South Africa, focuses on linking communities and businesses in developing land. The underpinning theme of partnership in design and delivery is one which can be seen with regard to other areas as part of this initiative, such as tourism. The Lukhanji Local Municipality within the Chris Hani District in Eastern Cape has seen the successful use of partnership arrangements, in governance and business, in furthering its tourist industry (Eastern Cape Rural Development Agency, 2010). This partnership model has also been applied to rural renewal and renewal projects in several other projects in the Eastern Cape, such as Nkonkobe. This small town development focused on improving employment in the area and also raising basic living standards, helping people out of poverty. The area has local universities which are part of this project, and their role as partners working with communities and businesses as well as public offices, is to build on and develop agriculture, tourism, the government and social sector, and the business sector. These aims are driven by actors such as universities, farmers and local businesses, in partnership with local, public and government levels.

USA: North Dakota

There are several key actors engaged in governance and delivery of the rural renewal projects across the state of North Dakota, driven by the USDA and, within the USDA, the Rural Development arm (USDA RD). The USDA RD has three focuses in funding and delivering rural renewal projects across North Dakota: communities, families, and businesses. The rural renewal for funding in projects across North Dakota around these areas focuses on examples such as housing, healthcare, business development and the development of technological capacity and infrastructure. The USDA RD works with a range of local businesses and public organisations, and there is a strong focus on the participation of communities and the emphasis on partnership working across all these actors in governance and delivery of the rural renewal projects.

Responsibilities of a REAP Zone

- Conduct a citizen-led, comprehensive, long-term, strategic planning process for development of the community according to the principles of the Community Empowerment Initiative.
- Develop specific performance benchmarks and indicators from the strategic plan; enter into the Benchmark Management System and keep them current.
- Seek a broad range of resources to implement the strategic plan, with emphasis on mobilising local and regional resources that will continue to be available after the REAP Zone designation expires, rather than looking to USDA or other outside sources to subsidise local development.
- Obtain approval from USDA Rural Development before amending any of the community strategic plan elements, benchmarks, or performance measures.
- Provide USDA Rural Development with descriptions of successful practices that have potential application in other communities facing similar conditions and issues.
- Report regularly on the community progress in implementing its strategic plan through the Benchmark Management System and other reports as requested by USDA.
- Manage all funds used to implement the strategic plan responsibly and report publicly on their use and accomplishments; conduct annual independent audits of all funds used to implement the strategic plan, whether government or private.

- Recognise that the objective of the REAP Zone program is not merely project implementation, but community empowerment, and devote significant resources and attention to achieving this by building the skills of citizens and leaders to plan, implement, manage, and evaluate their own programs.
- Develop and maintain broad and open partnerships with other local and regional organisations that have a stake in the enhancement of the quality of life in the REAP Zone; these partnerships will become a bridge to establishing the permanent capability of the community to make continuing improvements without special Federal assistance after the REAP Zone designation expires.
- Remain faithful to the principles of the Community Empowerment Initiative that put strong emphasis on the critical importance of broad-based citizen participation in all phases of the development, implementation, and evaluation of the strategic plan, with special emphasis placed on welcoming those members of the community (minorities, low income citizens) who are traditionally left out of the process.

Source: www.rd.usda.gov/programs-services/businesses/rural-
economic-area-partnership-program-reap-zones

Within these strategic aims, there are a number of areas dedicated to business development and also agriculture and farming. There is also a large focus, related to each of these core areas of activity, on community economic development. Within the remit of economic community development, the key themes of the rural renewal initiative in East Dakota, driven by the USDA, are set out in the box below. These are focused on the expansion and development of businesses, public infrastructure and community interests.

The Community Economic Development encompasses programs and initiatives that assist communities and regions realise their long-term goals through provision of technical assistance and grants that supports strategic planning and community visioning in order to provide a foundation for economic development. Initiatives include:

- Regional Development Priority
- Stronger Economies Together
- Promise Zone Initiative
- Sustainable Rural Downtowns Case Studies
- Investing in Manufacturing Communities Partnership
- Rural Jobs Accelerator
- Rural Economic Area Partnership Program (REAP Zones)
- National Rural Development Partnership
- StrikeForce

Source: www.business.nd.gov/data/community/

Concluding remarks

This chapter has examined and summarised the key debates drawn from theory and practice across rural renewal examples, from a comparative national, sub-national and community level perspective. This chapter has also considered and reviewed the literatures in the sections above and identified the key themes in urban renewal projects. These areas of debate give rise to key substantive issues which need to be tackled in the research design. Each of the key literatures, such as public policy and governance, raises key research questions which need to be addressed. The theoretical framework of policy networks, drawn from governance literature set out in this chapter, has been used to examine the key actors in governance in each of the cases. The four empirical case study chapters, discussed in the latter sections of this chapter, each exhibit governance arrangements which focus on partnerships and networks in design and delivery. The research is informed equally by the grey literature from the four cases, in terms of theory and practice. The practical examples and this grey literature, as noted in the earlier sections of this chapter, are underpinned by partnership and network arrangements in governance. The discussion of governance theory in this chapter, focused on the role of governance networks and partnerships, and the interpretation of roles between the actors engaged in delivery of rural renewal in these partnerships, informs the next chapter. The next chapter will examine the way interpretivist governance and networks inform the empirical research in the four case study chapters. This will draw upon the scholarly debates and the practice settings of the four empirical case studies (discussed in this chapter). These will then be used to build models for interpretive governance which will be applied and tested in the case study chapters.

3 Roles and meanings in governance partnerships and networks

This chapter builds on the previous chapter by unpacking the key questions that have come from the governmental, theoretical and planning literatures detailed in the second chapter. The first sections of this chapter set out the hypothesis and research questions in detail, before moving on to the methods used in the research. The chapter will then conclude by setting out the interview questions, survey questions and ethics employed in field research in the case study areas. The sample taken in the case study areas will also be discussed, including respondents and non-respondents, before concluding with a discussion of the cases' institutional and cultural traits. It is to the institutional and governance context that we turn first.

Comparison: the institutional and governance context across the rural renewal cases

The influence of the institutional design of governance within the four case study areas is not the focus of the book, though evidently it exerts a large influence on the design of governance of the rural renewal programmes and has implications for their design and delivery, particularly in regard to the role of partnership governance and the agencification of delivery. For example, in federal systems such as the US (North Dakota), Australia (New South Wales) and South Africa (Eastern Cape), there are competencies at state or regional level which the centre does not deliver or manage. In devolved unitary settings, such as the Vale of Glamorgan case study in Wales, there are devolved functions and powers which rest with the Welsh Government (WG), and powers which rest with the UK government in Westminster. There are also supra national funding grants to which each of these rural renewal initiatives may apply, bringing with them an aspect of multi-level governance (through conditions attached to the funding, for example). The (devolved) unitary-federal debate in comparison shows these aspects of constraints, with the devolved unitary structure in the Vale's case meaning that there is greater clarity and 'fixed' powers when compared with the pre devolution unitary system, though these are obviously different to the federal system with the local or regional tier charged with various powers and competencies which can affect renewal initiatives, such as responsibility for areas like housing, transport and community representation. The distinction between unitary and federal systems in governance has been shown to influence the design of renewal programmes (Shand, 2013) through the extent of the local or regional tiers, and the number of decentralised agencies involved in the delivery of the projects. Where there are fewer competencies at the local or regional levels, we tend to see a greater number of agencies delivering projects on behalf of central government departments in renewal programmes. The success or failure of the renewal programmes may also be influenced by institutional design to an extent, as there is greater potential for confusion among the partners collaborating to deliver the projects if there is not an existing system of partnership. These types of issues – such as confusion in communication, targets or goals – are found in multi-agency working where there is a large number of actors who have not previously come together. Where roles and responsibilities are understood and interpreted correctly among the actors in the governance partnership, it is likely to frustrate the outcomes and delivery of the renewal projects to an extent, through competencies and interlocking function at federal or regional levels devolved from the national level through constitutions or conventions. However, despite this, we still see a large focus in design and delivery across the four rural renewal cases on the role of agencies:

> Perhaps reducing the need for ad hoc creation of large agencies in some cases to operate in governance networks and partnerships drawing on Elazar's (1997) centre-periphery model, it is possible to support his case by looking at the case study areas that federalism works as an enabling tool in the transition to networks. These differences in the case study architectures are expected to be relevant in the case study areas as institutional design traits, i.e. federalism promotes the management and communication channels necessary to facilitate the complex mesh of governance networks. This quality of federal structures, as Elazar rightly notes, is in stark contrast to the unitary structure and the resultant problems occurring when attempting to craft a model of network multi-actor governance, of shared responsibility and increased lines of accountability. Nor is this process of network governance divorced from institutions. It would be an exaggeration to claim that agencification is a form of creeping federalism or devolution, but it would be accurate to suggest, again following Elazar, that institutional practice is replicated in the ties in the governance network.
>
> (Shand, 2013: 31–32)

To be sure, across the rural renewal case studies focused on here there are several institutional points to consider: there are federal–unitary and devolved structural differences across the cases, and there are also the size and scope of the case study areas to consider. In comparing across these four rural renewal programmes, we see common themes such as the focus on community engagement in delivery, in underpinning notions of sustainability, and in the range of actors engaged in the composition of the partnership, drawn from the public, private and voluntary sectors.

The focus of the rural renewal programmes sets out to achieve both short-term and longer-term goals, driven by the need to develop areas like communications, businesses and public services. In governance across the four rural renewal cases, there is a focus on partnership, and the use of governance agencies in delivery to varying extents. The focus on partnerships and agencies across different institutional systems and traditions, including project funding from different levels of governance, creates an intriguing case for comparison. It is to the methodological approach in undertaking this comparison that the next sections now turn.

Constructivism and interpretive governance: methodological approach

The focus on interpretive governance in unpacking the partnership delivery is underpinned from the constructivist paradigm. The creation and understanding of roles (Howell, 2013: 29) among governance actors is premised upon interpretivism and the behavioural turn in governance and public administration. The methodological and theoretical roots of these approaches are focused on shared realities, locally constructed; in this case, the shared reality of the rural renewal programmes. However, the extent to which the constructions of this reality remain shared are subject to the vagaries of circumstance and, most crucially, the interpretations of this reality by the different actors in the governance delivery of these programmes. As Howell notes, 'Reality is locally constructed. Based on experience although shared by many. Dependent on person/group changeable' (Howell, 2013: 29). Methodologically, in terms of applying this approach, the roles and interpretations of the actors in governance of the rural renewal programmes, as well as the researcher, should combine to 'create a consensus through individual constructions including the construction of the investigator' (Howell, 2013: 29). These constructions of the actors and the investigator are then modelled in each case study chapter in the partnership governance model which is discussed elsewhere in this chapter.

In terms of behavioural and interpretive governance, this book follows Bevir and Rhodes in emphasising the approach of scholars such as Geertz in stating the role of the social sciences as not solely focused on finding laws, empirics and patterns; but rather in unpacking the meanings and motivations behind behaviours. Social science is 'not an experimental science in search of law but an interpretive one in search of meaning' (Geertz, 1993). This focus places the need to examine roles and interactions between actors in partnership or network governance as central to finding meaning. This theoretical focus on governance therefore lends itself to the ethnographic or story telling approaches in terms of the methods chosen and undertaken.

This book adopts the policy networks approach, focusing on the inter-pretations (Bevir and Rhodes, 2006), roles and power relations between the actors in design and delivery of the four rural renewal programmes in the cases. To be sure, the focus on partnerships as governance mechanisms makes some assumptions about the design of the governance mechanisms, however each of the rural renewal programmes employs terminology in the aims of the rural renewal programmes about partners and partnership; evidently these actors seem not to have equal access to resources, creating the focus on roles, interpretations and power relations across the governance arrangements in the cases.

Key research questions

Underpinned by the discussion of governance partnership and interpretive literature reviewed in the previous chapter, the key research questions are also drawn from the grey literature produced by the key actors in the cases. The notion of power and collaboration in the partnership delivery is likely to be affected by the extent of agencification and disaggregation from the centre in the partnership. The nature and effect of power relations in the policy networks approach involves the role of the centre, the power and function across the partnership in delivery, and the different models of power such as the differentiated power model (DPM) and the asymmetric power model (APM) which each examine the pattern of relations across the governance partnership in delivery (Marsh *et al.*, 2003). These discussions of power also have implications for the different roles of the actors in the partnership governing the rural renewal programmes across the four cases, with the role of funding and cooperation between the actors, such as communities and businesses, central in terms of how they work with the centre regarding power, function and delivery. The research questions are driven by such debates across both theory and practice in comparing these large-scale rural renewal programmes, and the emphasis on the role of col-laboration between actors across tiers of governance, government agencies, communities and businesses, collaborating in governance partnerships in the four case studies' rural renewal programmes.

Within these partnerships, there are a number of issues which can potentially arise which underpin power relations and collaborations: problems of communication and of tensions between actors. The large number of projects in the four rural renewal programmes and the subsequent targets in these projects mean there is potential for problems in collabora-tion and delivery, given the large number of projects involved in the over-arching rural renewal programmes. The communication across actors equally may reflect the power relations between actors in the governance partnership, such as the flow of resources from an actor to the rest of the actors in the partnership. In addition, roles and interpretations across the governance partnerships may affect delivery of the rural renewal projects. The role of major actors such as the central government department in the policy network, and/or the funder(s) of the projects, is likely to affect the behaviour and collaboration between the actors in the partnership. Evidently, though there is a large focus in each of the four case study areas on partnership delivery in the governance of rural renewal projects, the power relations between actors raise questions around whether the governance delivery mechanism can be couched as a partnership, or whether there are inequalities and power relations at work among the actors.

Hypothesis

The hypothesis is, therefore, that power relations and roles in the notion of partnerships are constructed and driven by the funding and resource awarding bodies.

The key research questions examined in the case study areas are:

1   Partners or networks: roles, power and who governs?
2   What is the role of communities in the rural renewal projects?
3   Who are the relevant stakeholders in the rural renewal projects?
4   Who drives funding and delivery in the rural renewal projects?

These questions reflect key issues of cooperation and power relations across governance partnerships and the meaning of roles within these governance partnerships. The conscious or unconscious role ascribed to the actors in partnership is not a function of their willingness in their new role (or indeed how popular or unpopular they may feel in presenting innovative ideas) but rather an inescapable assumption. As Bevir notes: 'Students of culture concentrate on the meanings conveyed by patterns of behaviour, forms of social organization, economic systems ... when people act, they do so in accord with their conscious, preconscious, or unconscious beliefs' (Bevir, 2011: 295). Drawing upon Wittgenstein, Bevir argues that people's conceptions are based upon webs of belief. Webs of belief are cultural constructions based on inherited thought; 'people reach the webs of belief they do against the background of inherited traditions' (Bevir, 2011: 299). This kind of inherited construction of roles is one which operates in and on the actors in the governance partnership.

Within this context, the actors in the governance partnership role is constructed as an individual who should innovate and embrace new opportunities in areas of pedagogy such as actors in the governance partnership, often in the company of several similar individuals, reinforcing the construction of the actors in the governance partnership role as one of innovation and experiment, through mutual role recognition (Mead, 1934; Bevir, 2009). The actors in the governance partnership construct their roles in the partnership through mutual recognition. In this manner, a mutual role recognition and reinforcement implementation takes place, constructing the roles of actors in the governance partnership. This kind of inherited construction of roles is one which operates in and on the individual. Both the institution and the role have meaning, and memory. As discussed earlier, part of this is tradition or inherited thinking and inherited meaning, and these ghosts assert influence on the role and, through this, the individual as they offer unavoidable constructions and interpretations of the role throughout the history of the office.

The notion of governance as storytelling draws upon Sorensen's (2014) idea of political storytelling by political leaders. Sorensen argues that discourses in governance disseminated by leaders of change, funding or character, for example, tell stories about the individual and the role. These stories shape the view of the individual in the role (though, it should be pointed out, this is not a phenomena restricted to governance, as any recently sacked football manager would attest). However, the importance of storytelling is not just to create narratives of the actor in the role at that time, but to create stories of legacy and historical importance; this is a way of living up to the predecessors in the role. This is important because the weight of the role drives actors to perform, and to live up to the role and their predecessors (Sorensen, 2002). By applying Sorensen's idea of this storytelling by political leaders to the idea of governance as theatre, we can see storytelling allows leaders engaged in governance to create their own histories or moments in the roles, through speeches, soundbites, or connections.

Within this context, the individual's role is constructed as an individual who should innovate and embrace new opportunities in areas of policy making and delivery, often in the company of several similar individuals, reinforcing the construction of the individual's role as one of innovation and experiment, through mutual role recognition (Mead, 1934; Bevir, 2009). The individual constructs the role of innovator through mutual recognition; by discussing, as our individual case studies in this essay did, new ideas and sharing practice. In this manner, a mutual role recognition and reinforcement implementation takes place constructing the individual not as an innovative and experimental policy maker. Rather than simply offer reflections, we assert that our argument, five propositions, contains examples of these happenings in practice, with real policy consequences and effects. As we note earlier in this book, the focus of our argument is not institutionalism(s); rather it is the effect of memory, traditions and echoes on the individual. These effects mean that the individual's interpretation of their own role and others around them (and likewise, others of their own and indeed others) is skewed in their construction, due to the pressure of these effects. The business of the role, then, merely becomes a part in a play; an actor assuming a headline role for a tour, under the continuous reminders and pressures of their role.

The effect of role interpretation and of governance as theatre is further illustrated by the role of multi-agency working. Drawing on policy failures in partnership governance and the multi-agency delivery that underpinned it, there are examples of role interpretation that constrained the effectiveness of policy delivery and the joined-up nature of the multi-agency system. These issues were, alongside other problems, caused by role interpretation: problems of communication, clarity and stress. Further problems created by the problem of role interpretation – and the weight of roles on actors – were those of lack of coherence and trust between the actors in the multi-agency setting. Additionally, the role of multi-agency and network or partnership delivery in governance settings has grown rapidly in the last 20 years, giving rise to changes in the role perception of officials and actors. An example of this is given in research by Sorensen (2002) where she examines the role of Danish municipal politicians, who, like many holders of political office, are embedded in working with multi agency networks. Sorensen argues that the role of these officials has shifted from politicians to metagovernors, enmeshed in and overseeing a complex network of decision-making, power and delivery, as 'no single actor is capable of governing society. Governance today is a complex and interactive process' (Sorensen, 2006: 107). The role of networks and partnerships in governance increases the number of roles and the tendency for role interpretation to affect outcomes in policy. The weight of these roles and these consequences for delivery emphasise the importance of role interpretation in complex governance settings.

Methodological instruments: applying the method and governance approaches

Comparing governance design and delivery

The following sections of the chapter discuss the underpinning themes which will inform the research conducted across the four rural renewal case study areas and the broader central research questions set out above. These themes will be instruments employed across each of the four empirical case study chapters. These themes are designed to provide an overview of key themes across each of the four empirical case study areas, taking into account that key terms have differing meanings across these areas. These themes are selected to reflect the roles, in design and delivery, of the different actors which comprise governance mechanisms in the rural renewal programmes in the cases. These actors include national and local levels, community actors, and private sector interests, the third sector, planners and those from agencies. The key themes were constructed from analysis of the literature, policy documents regarding regeneration nationally, and more specific local authority and agency driven publications.

The role of differing meanings

These key themes in each case study chapter each have a governance component in terms of which bodies, businesses and agencies are (or were) engaged in the delivery of regeneration, where funding is allocated, and where co-operation between these different bodies takes place. The key underpinning themes and questions, which will inform the broader central research questions, are set out below:

- Is the organisation is heavily involved in the policy process?
- Does the rural renewal initiative have too many or too few stakeholders?
- Do you feel there has been a good leadership-in term of direction of projects, accountability – in the renewal imitative?
- What role do communities play in the process?
- Does this happen in an informal or formal manner?
- Does this happen more in terms of budgets, formulation or implementation?
- Who allocates budgets for the projects?
- How are projects chosen?
- Who are the main bodies and partners involved in delivery of rural renewal?

Building the network interpretivist model

As discussed in the preceding literature review chapter, the interpretivist framework is grounded in the notion of roles and meanings. In governance settings, these are often highlighted in the design and delivery of projects (in these cases, rural renewal programmes). As discussed at length in the previous chapter, the extent of governance networks and partnerships is highly prevalent, both in large-scale projects and in community-focused policies, or in the delivery of local and national public service provision. The model below is designed to annotate the process of interpretivism in governance: crucially, the construction and interpretation of roles in these partnership and network arrangements is central to how the constituent partners view themselves, each other and their respective roles in delivery. The two figures below attempt to annotate this theoretical notion by illustrating it as a process.

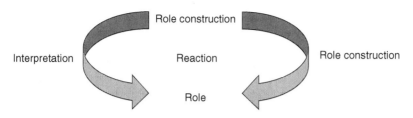

Figure 3.1 Roles and interpretations in governance networks and partnerships.

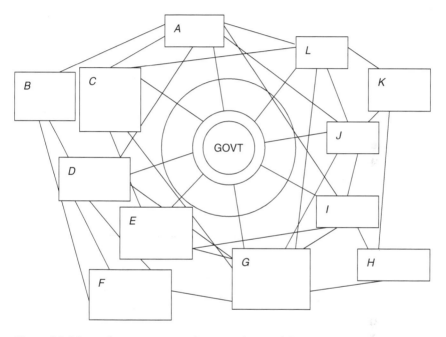

Figure 3.2 Network governance and partnership model.

Applying the models to the cases: governance, networks and interpretation

The model in Figure 3.2 is designed to show the roles and responsibilities of the different actors in the governance of rural renewal programmes. Across the four case study areas, the literature produced by government departments, governance agencies and community groups or businesses in the areas demonstrate a consistent approach to partnership working in design across the four cases, as discussed in the previous literature review chapter. The literature discussed in Chapter 2 also emphasises the importance of coordination through approaches like New Public Governance and multi-agency working. However, the much broader issue of network governance approaches also has implications for the network governance model in Figure 3.2. The question of roles and the understanding of these roles are important issues in the obstacles to collaborative arrangements (whether seen as network or partnership driven). Equally, the issues of communication, differing targets and competition among actors are all aspects which affect the successful delivery of policy and projects. The network model in Figure 3.2 has been previously used to examine the network governance approach to the design and delivery of large-scale urban renewal programmes in the UK, Germany and the USA (Shand, 2013). In this book, the application of the same network governance model as a template to the four cases of rural renewal will examine the role of partnerships in delivery. The key themes and questions set out in Chapter 1 – and then discussed in more depth earlier in this chapter – are set out to examine the role of actors in governance and delivery. The key themes of rural renewal programmes are reflected in the questions: namely, who is funding the projects, the role of communities, and the underpinning issues of sustainability in the projects.

The model draws upon the policy networks approach, emphasising the role of interpretation in these networks. The key actors, funding and decision making, and delivery are key aspects in modelling the governance of the rural renewal cases across the Vale of Glamorgan, the Eastern Cape, North Dakota, and New South Wales. The governance model of delivery in these cases will examine the roles of the actors in governance, with the design of partnerships across the cases including a range of cross sectoral partners – the roles, powers and functions of the actors in these governance models are reflected in the partnership governance model above. The model set out above is the framework, and, in each of the four rural renewal case study areas, the model will then be populated to annotate the relations between the actors in partnership, following the examination of the governance relations between the actors and the delivery of the projects across the four rural renewal programmes.

This model illustrates the ideal type network governance model, designed by governments in the cases. This model illustrates the actors in the cases as co-ordinated and non-hierarchical. This is shown in this initial model of the ideal type network by the lines connecting each of the others to one another. The lines are of equal thickness and are unbroken to emphasise the ideal of co-ordination between actors rather than hierarchical exchange relations across actors. This model will be tested against the hypothesis and findings, and the real – world models set out in the empirical chapters. The governance model above illustrates the flow of relations between actors in the regeneration initiatives. Drawing on the hypothesis, the dominance of some actors in the network would impose an asymmetrical dimension in terms of governance in the case study areas. This is reflected in the model above, with the flow of relations coming from the centre through the tiers of actors. This is shown by the connecting lines. The thickness and direction of the lines in this model will indicate the existence of asymmetries or otherwise.

(Shand, 2013: 27)

Concluding remarks

This chapter has set out the theoretical and methodological approaches which underpin the book and the examination of the four rural renewal case study areas. The practice focus on partnership governance, both in design and delivery, across the four rural renewal cases is reflected in the theoretical manner these themes are examined. This approach focuses on the processes of funding, coordination and outcomes in the rural renewal case study areas, and the interaction between the actors in the governance partnership in delivering the projects in rural renewal. The role of interpretative governance is also a key theoretical focus of the book in examining the interaction between the different partners in delivery of rural renewal and the effect this interaction, in terms of resources, communications and power relations, has in terms of the outcomes of the rural renewal programmes in the four cases.

Comparing across the cases, the role of governance partnerships and the focus on communities come across as clear key themes of each of the four rural renewal cases, though these need to be couched in the broader context of national and regional governance. In terms of comparison, institutional settings are not the focus of the book though they evidently have a large influence on the ability of the partners, or the central government, to design governance delivery of such large-scale renewal and delivery programmes. The federal–unitary debate exerts influence on the competencies that are divided between the central, regional or local level, and also exerts constraints on, for example, how many decentralised delivery agencies are involved in the partnership, competency at regional or local level around funding allocation, and the role of communities.

4 UK

Vale of Glamorgan

This chapter examines the first empirical case study. This UK case study, in the Vale of Glamorgan, is driven by key partnerships involving the agricultural, business, governmental and educational sectors. The partnership is focused on businesses in the region and existing strengths, working towards tourism and farming in particular, and an emphasis on community participation and voice in the design, implementation and bidding for funding process. These processes embed the community and local businesses through much of the rural renewal projects in the area. This takes place not only through some aspects of consultation – an aspect of governance design and delivery seen in other large-scale rural (and urban) renewal initiatives – but through board representation in awarding funding for projects, in bidding for this funding and in aspects of the delivery of the projects themselves. This has implications for the governance of the rural renewal initiative, as the community, local businesses and the local authority appear to be some of the main actors both in terms of governance design and delivery in the Vale. This chapter begins by examining the socio-economic context for rural renewal in the Vale of Glamorgan, before moving on to set out an overview of the projects, through progress, funding and outcomes. The chapter then moves on to conceptualise the projects in terms of governance, with particular regard to the role of communities, role interpretation and the power relations in governance design and delivery, examining the roles and relations between the major and more peripheral actors in governance.

> There is broad agreement both in Wales and across the United Kingdom that regeneration is a comprehensive process involving a range of organisations, which aims to tackle a combination of social, economic, physical and environmental issues and that it is focused on areas of disadvantage, particularly those where the market alone cannot deliver improvement.
> (www.valeofglamorgan.gov.uk/en/our_council/council/vale_
> facts_and_figures/vale_facts_and_figures.aspx, 2015)

Rural renewal across the Vale of Glamorgan: the demographic and social context

The social and demographic context for rural renewal across the Vale of Glamorgan is reflected in the area. Different aspects of the rural renewal programme focus on the development of town centres, public services, tourism and agriculture. These projects encompass the scale of renewal across the Vale including the linkage between urban and rural development through the growth of local businesses and tourism across the more rural areas in terms of landscape and beaches:

> It covers 33,097 hectares (130 square miles) with 53 kilometres of coastline, of which 19 kilometres is Heritage Coast. The main settlements are Barry, Penarth, Llantwit Major, Dinas Powys and Cowbridge. Barry, the largest town with a population of approximately 51,000, is the Vale's administrative centre, a seaside resort and port. Four miles to the west of the town centre, at Rhoose is Cardiff International Airport.
>
> (www.valeofglamorgan.gov.uk/en/our_council/council/vale_
> facts_and_figures/vale_facts_and_figures.aspx, 2015)

One of the pressures the rural renewal initiative across the Vale faces is that of a rising population which will evidently require, from a governance perspective, greater resources and a focus on the longer term development of infrastructure and civic facilities across the Vale. In addition, the rural renewal projects emphasise the need to retain talent in the area, to develop existing business strength such as tourism and agriculture, and to attract people to live, work and visit the area. The rising population across the Vale of Glamorgan additionally has implications for the age of the growing number of residents:

> Based on the 2013 mid-year estimate (June 2014), the population of the Vale is estimated at 127,159 and according to the 2011-based Welsh Government projection the population is expected to continue rising but at a slower rate than that of the last 10 years. The 2011 Census estimated number of households in the Vale is 53,500 and the latest Welsh Government household projections (2011-based) indicate that this number will continue to grow, to an expected 61,052 households by 2036. The Welsh Government population projections (2011-based) also indicate that the age profile of the Vale is also expected to change; the number of children (age 0–15) is forecast to peak at 23,850 in 2023 before reducing to 21,893 in 2036 whilst the number of people aged 65+ will increase by more than 60% from 23,226 in 2011 to 38,473 in 2036. The population density of the Vale of

Glamorgan is an average of 3.83 people resident per hectare according to the 2011 Census which is higher than the national average (Wales) of 1.5.

(www.valeofglamorgan.gov.uk/en/our_council/council/vale_ facts_and_figures/vale_facts_and_figures.aspx, 2015)

The area of the Vale of Glamorgan, and the growing population, is reflected across the constituent areas that make up the Vale. The area of Barry, as will be discussed in the projects sections later on in this chapter, is one of important focus in the rural renewal programme in terms of developing the town centre and local business infrastructure. The population makeup of the towns across the Vale of Glamorgan is shown in Table 4.1.

In terms of how the demographic and social context across the Vale drives the focus of the rural renewal projects, there are a number of key underpinning social issues, such as the need to improve the level of educational attainment across the Vale, and the related issues of improving the level of employability in the area. Each of these are key social and public policy needs, both in terms of attracting people to stay and move to the Vale, and in achieving improving outcomes in the short as well as the longer term:

There are 23 electoral wards in the Vale of Glamorgan and of these the eight considered to be rural cover approximately 80% of the area. There are 79 Lower Super Output Layers which have an average population of around 1,600 people. The Welsh Government Annual Population Survey (December 2013), indicated that 15.9% (19,300) of the Vale's population over the age of 3 could speak Welsh. The unemployment rate (Job Seekers Allowance claimants as a percentage of working age population) in the Vale was 2.2% in August 2014 (compared to a

Table 4.1 Population of towns – 2011 Census

Town	Population
Barry	51,502
Penarth	22,083
Llantwit Major	10,621
Dinas Powys	7,799
Cowbridge	6,180
Rhoose	6,907
St Athan	4,495
Sully	4,543
Wenvoe	2,659

Source: www.valeofglamorgan.gov.uk/en/our_council/council/vale_facts_and_figures/vale_facts_ and_figures.aspx, 2015.

rate of 3.0% in August 2013). Within the Vale the highest rates were found in Barry, particularly in the wards of Castleland (5.7%), Court (5.2%), Gibbonsdown (4.7%), Buttrills (3.9%) and Cadoc (3.4%). Employment is characterised by a high proportion of people in the service sector. Compared with the rest of South East Wales, the Vale has a lower proportion of manufacturing jobs and a higher proportion in distribution, hotels and catering. The number of VAT registered businesses in 2008 was 3,165 (revised, up from 3,145 in 2007). The Vale of Glamorgan Council employs 5,457 full-time and part-time employees (as at March 2014) and in 2011–12 the Council's gross revenue expenditure was in excess of £340 million, which equates to £2,720 per resident.

(www.valeofglamorgan.gov.uk/en/our_council/council/vale_
facts_and_figures/vale_facts_and_figures.aspx, 2015)

Additionally, the rural renewal programme emphasises the role of partnership in governance, through design, management and delivery. The partnership approach in governing the rural renewal programme across the Vale encompasses actors from the public, private and third sectors, and builds upon existing partnerships working across the Vale. The notion of partnership working in governance is one that the local authority is engaged in across several areas of delivery, working with a range of actors in the delivery of public and social services. This approach is, as we have seen in the preceding chapters, one that has been widely drawn upon in both rural and urban renewal initiatives:

The Council works in partnership with many different agencies in the public, voluntary and business sectors to deliver a wide range of services. Commuting patterns in the Vale of Glamorgan in 2011 showed that there was a net outward migration of 12,100 workers (29,500 people commuting out of the local authority area to work compared to 17,400 commuting into the local authority area to work). The close proximity of the capital city will always have an impact on the working location of Vale of Glamorgan residents, but these figures suggest that there is scope for businesses and employers to employ local residents if new jobs were available. In respect of pupil attainment, the Vale remains one of the highest performing education authorities in Wales with 65.7% of pupils achieving 5 or more GCSE grades A*, the highest percentage of the 22 Welsh local authorities in 2009–2010 (currently approximately 14% of the population are of school age). Similarly, health indicators for the Vale are generally good compared to other parts of Wales.

(www.valeofglamorgan.gov.uk/en/our_council/council/vale_
facts_and_figures/vale_facts_and_figures.aspx, 2015)

Drawing upon the statistics and social context set out above, the rural renewal projects across the Vale are evidently concerned with very wide-ranging aims. In common with many renewal programmes, there is a focus on both public and private sector development, and a twin aim to achieve both short-term goals and, in the longer term, in ensuring these social- and business-focused outcomes are sustainable and embedded. The following sections now move on to focus on the key project areas across rural renewal in the Vale.

Vale of Glamorgan rural renewal initiative

The Vale of Glamorgan rural renewal programme covers, in fact, both urban and rural areas, such as the key areas of Barry, town centres and business districts. This chapter now moves on to examine the focus on the differing rural renewal projects and key elements of the programme, which centres on the following project areas. The projects are discussed in greater detail in the latter sections of this chapter:

- Barry Island Regeneration
- The Pumphouse
- The Former Lifeguard Building
- The Former Tourism Information Centre
- High Street/Broad Street
- S106 Play Areas
- Castleland Renewal Area (includes the Upper Holton Road and shop front renewal project)
  (www.valeofglamorgan.gov.uk/en/working/regeneration/Vibrant-and-Viable-Places-Programme-of-Investment-2014-2017.aspx)

Overview of key projects and partners

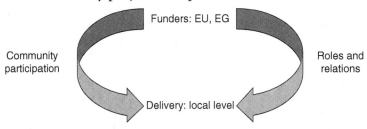

Figure 4.1 Roles and interpretations in governance networks and partnerships in the Vale of Glamorgan.

Institutional context

In terms of institutional design, the key actors in driving and funding the projects are the national (Welsh Government) level, with prior European level funding. This demonstrates the important role of the national level in steering the constituent rural renewal projects to the coordinated national agenda, as will be discussed in later sections of this chapter. The priorities, funding and setting of the governance partnership are driven by the national level, though working closely with the local authority and the community in decision making and awarding of funds for projects, setting the context of the roles of the actors –notably the community – engaged in delivery of the rural renewal projects.

The devolved nature of the Vale case study perhaps allows greater cooperation between the national and local levels, without the creation of large-scale agencies in delivery. The important role of the community actor in the governance partnership is a vital one in terms of role construction and participation, and does impact upon the governance and power relations and respective roles which are then ascribed by the national rather than state level, and the construction of roles and the rules of engagement within the policy network. The roles of the other actors in the partnership are constructed by the role of national and local levels of government as the key decision makers and funders, notably as the local level is engaged in partnership working in a range of areas.

Vale of Glamorgan Local Development Plan

The Vale of Glamorgan Local Development Plan (LDP) sets out a specific vision of governance of rural renewal in the Vale, prioritising the role of communities and partnerships in delivery. The role of communities in the design and delivery of rural renewal projects across the Vale of Glamorgan is driven by national and local concerns. The need to enshrine the role of communities is central to the national and local conception of the delivery of the programme: 'The Delivery Agreement that has been approved by the Welsh Government contains a Community Involvement Scheme (CIS) which sets out the Council's approach to community and stakeholder involvement and engagement throughout the LDP process' (Vale of Glamorgan Local Development Plan 2011–2026, 2013: 5). The emphasis in the LDP is on the role of communities, of creating sustainable structures to deliver into the longer term the rural renewal projects' aims and to create evaluation mechanisms to examine progress of projects, engagement of communities and outcomes in rural renewal across the Vale. Drawing upon the national level, the LDP focuses upon several key planning elements of national policy setting. The key focuses of the LDP are the *Environment Strategy for Wales* (2006), *The Wales Spatial Plan* (2008), *The Wales Transport Strategy* (2008) and policy directives focused on areas such as communities, health and physical wellbeing. However, a key focus in terms of governance design and delivery of rural renewal is the integration of the national-level policy framework *Economic Renewal: A New Direction* (2010), which sets out the national priorities in Wales for economic development. These key themes are 'investing in high quality sustainable infrastructure; making Wales a more attractive place to do business; broadening and deepening the skills base; encouraging innovation; and targeting support for business' (Vale of Glamorgan Local Development Plan 2011–2026, 2013: 10). These aims map on to the Vale of Glamorgan LDP and the rural renewal projects design and governance. The span of projects across the Vale includes key themes and focus on areas such as developing businesses around tourism – both for landscape and beaches – farming and agriculture, public services and infrastructure such as education and healthcare, community engagement and town centre development. At the local level, the LDP sets out a number of aims for these key areas. For example, these national policy strategy areas are reflected at the local level in the Vale through development plans for ecology, transport and housing, each of which is reflected in the aims of the rural renewal programme. The LDP also emphasises several key objectives which are reflected in the design and delivery of rural renewal. These are:

- To sustain and further the development of sustainable communities within the Vale of Glamorgan, providing opportunities for living, learning, working and socialising for all.
- To ensure that development within the Vale of Glamorgan makes a positive contribution towards reducing the impact of and mitigating the adverse effects of climate change.
- To reduce the need for Vale of Glamorgan residents to travel to meet their daily needs and enabling them greater access to sustainable forms of transport.
- To protect and enhance the Vale of Glamorgan's historic, built, and natural environment.
- To maintain, enhance and promote community facilities and services in the Vale of Glamorgan.
- To reinforce the vitality, viability and attractiveness of the Vale of Glamorgan's town, district, local and neighbourhood shopping centres.
- To provide the opportunity for people in the Vale of Glamorgan to meet their housing needs.
- To foster the development of a diverse and sustainable local economy that meets the needs of the Vale of Glamorgan and that of the wider South East Wales Region.
- To create an attractive tourism destination with a positive image for the Vale of Glamorgan, encouraging sustainable development and quality facilities to enrich the experience for visitors and residents.

- To ensure that development within the Vale of Glamorgan uses land effectively and efficiently and to promote the sustainable use and management of natural resources.

(Vale of Glamorgan Local Development Plan 2011–2026, 2013: 24–27)

These key themes are embedded across the projects for rural renewal in the Vale. For example, the role of ecology is linked to sustainable transport measures and reducing the need for communities to travel. This involves the development of local business and aspects of production in areas such as agriculture. The creation of new jobs in the area also reduces the need for residents to travel, encourages people to remain in and move to the area, and facilitates tourism across the Vale. These aims are not unusual in renewal (both urban and rural) programmes, though are more pressing and difficult to achieve in rural areas. To strike a balance between ecological protection, house building and sustainable development of land is difficult, and one that requires the community to be engaged. As the community is flagged as a key partner in the LDP (and in the subsequent governance of the rural renewal projects), this provides a means of accountability and involvement in prioritising projects which will deliver greater numbers of housing, for example. In addition, the aims of increasing ecology, tourism, transport infrastructure and educational provision and attainment in the area are all community facing objectives, and the role of the community as partner in delivery is a crucial aspect of design in the governance of the programme. This is also reflected in the role of creative rural communities in the delivery of the projects, to which we turn in the following section.

Who drives funding and delivery in the rural renewal projects? Evaluating the projects

The projects are focused, as discussed above, on a number of key themes. In evaluating the progress and success of these projects, and therefore the success of achieving rural renewal more broadly across the Vale, there are a number of key factors to be evaluated. First, the aims of the programme: in renewal programmes these can at times be over ambitious or too long term, mitigating against community engagement. The branding and visibility of the programme has also been shown to be an important factor in achieving the goals of renewal programmes, especially where community involvement is a key aim (Shand, 2013). Second, the costs of projects and the success of outcomes are evidently key factors which need to be evaluated, and will be key drivers in determining the extent of success or failure in achieving the aims of the projects. Third, there is governance design, particularly the overarching aims of the rural renewal programme of achieving partnership governance in delivery of the projects, and in joining together actors from the supra and national levels (as funders), the local level, the local action group, and a range of local businesses as well as public and voluntary sector actors. Fourth, and finally, the rural renewal programme in the Vale emphasises the role of communities as partners, so this aspect of governance is also an important factor in evaluation. Of course, it should be remembered that in conducting any evaluation, the aims of the programme are both short and longer term, focused on achieving both sustainability and longer-term development.

An evaluation of the rural renewal programme in the Vale of Glamorgan was published by Ash Futures in 2015. This report focused on evaluating the Rural Development Programme (RDP) in the Vale. This included assessments of spending, of meeting the outcomes and targets the projects aimed for, and of the role of governance and delivery – particularly of partnerships – in the Vale's rural renewal programme. The report emphasised the partnership focus in bringing together the community, public and private development, and the Vale of Glamorgan Advisory Board, emphasising the role and function of communities in terms of the design and delivery of rural renewal projects across the Vale. The Vale's Advisory Board and The Creative Rural Communities (CRC) also demonstrate an important emphasis on the community role in achieving engagement in the design and delivery of the governance structure of the rural renewal projects across the Vale.

Who are the relevant stakeholders in the rural renewal projects? Rural renewal in the Vale of Glamorgan projects, funding and progress

In any renewal initiative, there is a delicate balance to be struck between achieving goals over the short term and a much longer, more sustainable focus on embedding facilities or changing behaviours, or maintaining funding and/or participatory streams. In the Vale, a number of small projects have benefitted from grants, funding and a focus on key themes within the area that are already successful, such as agriculture. The rural renewal programme, however, has also sought – and with a large amount of success – to develop these areas of success, particularly in investing in farming and agriculture across the Vale of Glamorgan and in developing tourism in the area. The resultant projects have both short-term gains and much longer-term aims. These ideals involve embedding these improved infrastructures but also in facilitating community voice and participation.

Projects: an overview of these is set out in Table 4.2. However, it must be noted that this is only an overview of the projects in the Vale, as there are several on-going and a myriad of micro level projects. The projects Table 4.2 focuses upon were selected as they reflect the key themes of the Vale of Glamorgan rural renewal programme, such as agriculture, tourism

Table 4.2 Outcomes and funding of projects in the Vale of Glamorgan

Project	Time period	Funder(s)	Cost (£)	Outcome
Local Housing Strategy	2014–2019	VoG		The Vale of Glamorgan Council has prepared a draft Local Housing Strategy 2014–2019 that sets out the vision for housing in the next five years. Between 1 September and 28 September 2014 the Council sought the views of residents, stakeholders, partners and colleagues with regard to the strategic direction for housing in the Vale and the content of the draft strategy.
Cardiff Airport Enterprise Zone	2014–	WG	2.75 million	The Welsh Government has commissioned a firm of consultants (AMEC) to progress a Development Framework for the entire zone area, to take in St Athan, the airport and surrounding land. The timescale for the production of the framework is late autumn 2014. The purpose of the framework will be to increase interest and also guide potential investors. In terms of infrastructure improvements, the Minister has previously announced that she will fund improvements to Five Mile Lane. The Council has established a Project Board to take the project forward and manage the processes leading up to and during a planning application/potential Compulsory Purchase Order. The Welsh Government is also keen to improve the Gileston to Old Mill section of the highway network to enhance access to the Enterprise Zone. Money has been provided by the Welsh Government since 2011/2012 to allow the Council to progress this scheme with a £2.75 million grant to progress the construction phase of the scheme given on October 2013. Work is well advanced on site and completion of the scheme is due in late 2014/early 2015. The Vale of Glamorgan Council submitted a bid in September 2013 to the UK Government to request parts of the county be granted Assisted Area status. After two periods of consultation the Government submitted its draft to the European Commission, including the St Athan, Rhoose and Peterston Super Ely wards of the Vale of Glamorgan. The new map was subsequently approved earlier this year. The inclusion of the St Athan and Rhoose wards will facilitate investment in the Enterprise Zone, whilst the Peterston Super Ely ward includes the major business site at junction 34 of the M4 motorway.

continued

Table 4.2 Continued

Project	Time period	Funder(s)	Cost (£)	Outcome
Castleland Renewal Area	2014		1.76 million	Across the schemes completed in 2013/2014, a total investment of £1,760,847 has been made in the area to improve living conditions. 316 homes were completed under the Facelift Programme; the Arbed Phase 2 programme has funded upgraded/new central heating systems, installation of voltage optimisers, solar thermal hot water systems, and energy advice packs; energy efficiency improvements to 21 properties in the form of external wall insulation and new central heating systems has also been carried out. In addition, work began to implement the additional House in Multiple Occupation (HMO) licensing scheme in the area. All known HMO owners were contacted. At the end of March 2014, five licences were issued; eight properties are progressing through the licensing process; and, 11 were deemed to be exempt due to change in occupation. The Council is to receive indicative funding for area renewal activity in the three-year period 2014/2015–2016/2017. Through this funding opportunity, Cabinet approved a budget of £1.5 million in March 2014 to support the regeneration of Upper Holton Road with the aim of renewing the fabric of the front elevation of the buildings; improving the visual impact of the street; and improving the availability of affordable accommodation. Property owners in the area have been contacted and work should begin on site in late autumn 2014. To support community facilities, private investment was sourced for the external refurbishment of the 5th Barry Sea Scout Hall on Holton Road to enable its use to be extended to the local community. The Jehu Group has been appointed by Newydd Housing Association as the contractor to redevelop the former Barry Magistrates Court on Thompson Street. The locally based contractor started the £6.3 million redevelopment in October 2013 with the aim of moving tenants into completed homes in spring 2015. The redevelopment of the site will provide 52 much needed affordable houses and flats in the area as well as retail units.

Golau Caredig Extra Care Scheme	This redevelopment of the former Theatre Royal site on Broad Street by Hafod Care Association provides affordable independent living accommodation for people over 55 in the form of 42 purpose-built one- and two-bedroom flats. Individual care and support will be provided for the tenants via 'in house' domiciliary care and tenant support service. The £7.2 million scheme has been developed by Hafod Care Association, part of the Hendre Group, in partnership with the Vale of Glamorgan Council. The development also includes several communal facilities including a restaurant, hairdressers, laundrette and multi-use activity area, as well as a feature glass façade to the front staircase.
Communities First – Barry Cluster	The Barry Cluster consists of parts of Buttrills, Cadoc, Castleland, Court and Gibbonsdown wards. The total population of the Cluster area is 15,777. The Communities First programme is Welsh Government funded to the end of 2014/2015. Following a period of staff recruitment, the arrangements for the Barry Cluster came into being in 2013. A Partnership Board became operational in 2014 and includes residents and businesses from across the Cluster area. Additional grants have been secured for specialised projects. For example, funding of £60,000 has been obtained from the Pupil Deprivation Grant, for local schools to promote an innovative approach to encouraging youngsters to engage with science, technology, engineering and maths. Other projects have addressed health issues associated with poverty such as obesity and smoking, with very considerable take up. A key focus for the programme has been lifting people out of poverty by addressing employment opportunities. Success has been achieved working in partnership with major employers such as Admiral Insurance. In March and October of this year, a Jobs Fair took place in partnership with Job Centre Plus that saw a total of over 2,000 visitors attend.

continued

Table 4.2 Continued

Project	Time period	Funder(s)	Cost (£)	Outcome
Innovation Quarter – Hydraulic Pumphouse				The Hydraulic Pumphouse is a Grade II Listed vacant property located in the Innovation Quarter at The Waterfront Barry. The Hydraulic Pumphouse is the subject of a legal joint venture between the Council and Welsh Government. With Welsh Government consent the Council has exchanged contracts with a developer.
				The developer (D S Properties Ltd) submitted a planning application in August of this year for a mixed use development.
The Vale of Glamorgan Local Development Plan	2011–2026			Having carried out consultations during the latter part of 2013, on a replacement Deposit Local Development Plan, the Alternative Sites consultation stage closed on 1 May 2014. Some 1,386 individuals responded to the Deposit Plan consultation who made approximately 3,200 individual representations. Following the close of this consultation the Council's responses will be prepared for each of the representations received to the Deposit Plan consultation (some 15,000 pages) and to the Alternative Sites consultation. A further 1,730 individuals responded to the Alternative Sites consultation who made approximately 8,100 individual representations on the suggested 'alternative sites'. The Alternative Sites Representation Register was then published in July 2014. Early in 2015 a report will be presented to Council for approval (via Cabinet/Scrutiny/Planning Committee) outlining all of the Council's responses to all of the representations made at each of the consultations. This, together with any additional evidence to support the Local Development Plan (LDP), will then be presented to the Welsh Government in May 2015. It is currently anticipated that an Examination in Public will be held in late summer 2015, with the Plan being adopted in late 2016. Work on a Community Infrastructure Levy has continued alongside the LDP, and the Council's

			proposed charging regime will also be addressed through an Examination in Public. In this regard the timetable for the Community Infrastructure Levy will follow the Council's LDP timetable. It is also relevant that a number of significant development proposals that relate to LDP allocations have been submitted to the Council and these applications are being considered through the statutory planning process.
The Quays – Waterfront Barry	2015–	230 million	The Quays was awarded full planning approval by the Vale of Glamorgan Council in March 2012 and work has been continuing behind the scenes to prepare the 100-acre site for construction. In addition to around 2,000 new homes, the 10-year £230 million waterfront regeneration project also includes a vibrant commercial district with bars, cafes, shops and a new 32,000 sq. ft. ASDA supermarket. Later phases will see improvements to community and water sports facilities, new public open spaces, a new primary school for the area and an allocation of affordable housing. The first show homes are expected to be open in early 2015. The ASDA superstore is expected to bring around 300 new jobs and wider benefits to the community. The recruitment operation is expected to start in January 2015, in preparation for opening the doors to customers in spring 2015.
Barry Island	2014–		The Cabinet meeting on 16 June 2014 approved the draft Destination Action Plan (DAP) for the Vale of Glamorgan for consultation purposes. The DAP was the subject of this year's Business Breakfast event at the Vale of Glamorgan Show and findings will be reported to Cabinet before the end of 2014. In terms of implementation work, Barry Island continues to be the focus of targeted investment. At the end of March 2014, a loan agreement between the Welsh Government, the Council and the Waterfront Consortium was signed, together with a Section 106 Deed of Variation to bring forward the construction of the Barry Island Link Road. As a result it is now currently anticipated that the road will be constructed by summer 2015.

continued

Table 4.2 Continued

Project	Time period	Funder(s)	Cost (£)	Outcome
Work Programme				The Council delivers parts of the Department for Work and Pensions' Work Programme across the Vale of Glamorgan. Previously delivered by the Lifelong Learning Directorate, the project now sits in the Economic Development Unit. It has been more closely integrated with regeneration activities to support local long term unemployed individuals back into the workplace. The team is currently engaging with ASDA in respect of its new Waterfront store, and is identifying and preparing individuals as recruitment approaches. The team is approaching a celebration for securing employment for its 500th unique client since the start of the programme in June 2011.
Vibrant and Viable Places Tackling Poverty Fund	2014/2015– 2016/2017			In April 2014 the Minister for Housing and Regeneration announced that the Council would be eligible for £1 million in capital funding (known as the Tackling Poverty Fund) over the three financial years 2014/2015, 2015/2016 and 2016/2017. The Council received guidance on how to apply for this funding on 12 June 2014. A request for the use of emergency powers to submit an application was authorised on 23 June 2014 to coincide with the Welsh Government's deadline for submitting the application. There is a strong geographic correlation in Barry between areas of concentrated deprivation, areas of concentrated social housing and traditional shopping areas.

The Communities First Cluster Area is the cornerstone for regeneration activity in this area of Barry and the programme of projects identified in the Council's application reflects and responds to the Cluster area delivery plan through physical investment. In light of this and the guidance issued for local authorities, tackling poverty is therefore an important theme that weaves through the programme of projects approved by the Welsh Government in July of this year. Details of the successful application were reported to the Cabinet meeting on 28 July 2014. Highlights so far from year one of the programme (2014/2015) include the Town Centre – third sector hub being delivered by the Vale Centre for Voluntary Services and the Youth Partnership – service hub being delivered by the Barry YMCA.

Source: www.valeofglamorgan.gov.uk/en/our_council/council/vale_facts_and_figures/vale_facts_and_figures.aspx, 2015.

and community engagement, as well as developing existing and new small businesses in the area.

Funding: The funding for rural renewal projects is driven by grants awarded by the local level and the board. Of course, these projects also reflect the focus of the Welsh Government at the national level in the priorities set out earlier in this chapter. In making a case for an award, a project group or community has to engage with the bidding process, making a business case to the board for the scope of the project and why this is a workable suggestion. The board also encompasses community representation. In this vein, the community is engaged with the funding process both through board membership and through the bidding process, rather than merely at specific and discrete stages of the rural renewal programme; that is, not through consultation at, for example, formulation or implementation stages. The community is a vital part of the Vale of Glamorgan rural renewal process because of the programme's focus on such a large number of small projects embedded within the local community.

What is the role of communities in the rural renewal projects? Delivery and governance structure: community representation in delivery

A key feature of the governance and role of communities in rural renewal in the Vale is that the key drivers are not only composed of large governance agencies or large-scale investment from business, as is evident in several other renewal (both urban and rural) programmes. The focus in terms of budgets, delivery and coordination is centred on the local authority, in awarding initially European level funding and, subsequently, the national level. The role of the local level in coordinating rural renewal in the Vale is a crucial one, both in terms of governance structure and in terms of coordinating such a large number of projects, several of which involve existing and very micro scale projects.

The governance structure put into place by the local authority is there to oversee the delivery of the projects and to act as a peer reviewer for funding applications from the constituent projects across the overarching rural renewal in the Vale of Glamorgan and Barry. This function is an important aspect of accountability, transparency and community engagement in the overarching delivery and governance of the projects. The board is composed of representatives from the communities and organisations engaged in the rural renewal programme, and acts as a check and balances type body in ensuring the voice of the community and the organisations – such as those residents or groups affected by the extent of success in the renewal projects. This awarding funding function of the board is one which allows the local authority to work with the communities engaged in the projects.

The focus in the Vale on long-term sustainability also seeks to develop the existing roles of tourism and agriculture in the Vale and surrounding area.

The need to attract tourism to the Vale is driven, evidently, by the desire to grow the local economy but also to plan land use in the area. The focus on developing – literally 'growing' – existing areas of agricultural expertise and industry in the Vale is also, as mentioned elsewhere in this book, crucial to both the short and longer-term success of the rural renewal programmes. The role of the board and the local authority in developing the existing economic strengths of the tourism and agriculture sectors in the Vale demonstrates partnership rather than a large unwieldy network, and also shows the importance of community integration in governance partnerships.

The notion of decision making in delivery – through board representation, oversight of the rural renewal projects, and funding awards – shows the partnership in decision making between the local authority and the board. However, this relationship should also be considered in terms of function and power in delivery. This is a complex question. Taking, for example, the funding that the board may award to groups who successfully bid to develop their projects, this has been awarded to the Vale of Glamorgan by, first, the European level and, more latterly, by the Welsh Assembly Government. This therefore shows the power dynamic between the actors – the organisation that is charged with awarding funding to actors in the rural renewal enjoys function rather than power. Though the act of awarding funding may be seen as one of power, the power still remains with the government, as the initial awarding body. For example, at the end of the lifetime of a funding cycle, the government is the actor most likely to have power over funding allocation, while the local authority would have to bid. However, the focus here should be on engagement, rather than on function and power.

Looking at the preponderance of renewal initiatives, rural and urban, across different countries which emphasise the role of partnership or network governance in design and delivery (as discussed in Chapter 2), the question of community engagement is a crucial one. In many of these programmes – just as in all four rural renewal cases examined in this book – there is a focus on community involvement. The Vale of Glamorgan example of community representation in both the delivery (in overseeing projects) and the role of both peer reviewer and awarding body demonstrates the community is engaged in the rural renewal projects throughout the process. This collaboration and coordination takes place from formulation, through the progress of projects, and in funding, delivery and the sustainability of the rural renewal projects.

In terms of the main actors, the local authority works with in delivering the rural renewal initiative, the community and the representative board are highly important in coordinating the different projects and strands of rural renewal in the Vale. This is indicative of more partnership working than a broader network and, conceptually, shows some innovative and participatory features. In applying governance frameworks such as the policy networks approach, we can see some disaggregation and asymmetry but also, more importantly, negotiation and consultation, through the engagement of the community and the creation by the local authority of the board discussed in the sections above. The local authority, itself removed from the centre and national decision-making (in this case, allocation of funding), has further decentralised the decision-making process to the board. This is not to negate the local level in the process of oversight, but rather to emphasise the capacity of the board in community representation and involvement throughout the process of governing the projects, rather than mere consultation at the formulation or implementation stages. In this instance, the disaggregation serves to increase transparency and to limit the asymmetric nature of partnerships. Moreover, the question of delivery of whether the rural renewal programme takes place in a partnership rather than a network is again supported by the Local Action Group. The Local Action Group is a partnership with the local level and is representative of the community. Within this arrangement, there is a fundamental question of power and function, most evidently driven by funding and resources. In addition, these organisations engaged in the delivery of projects do not have the same degree of funding or resources, or indeed role. The local level has the role of administrative or lead body and employs staff in the governance and delivery of rural renewal. The local level may then award funding grants to actors delivering projects or pilot projects, and these funds are provided both in terms of funding required and to pay for staff needed by the organisation to design and deliver the rural renewal project. Again, the questions of role and power are central to the design of the partnership arrangement, with the local authority maintaining the lead role in delivery and oversight. However, this should not detract from the important role of community representation. The interpretive nature of these roles not only embeds community representation in decision-making and governance in the Vale's rural renewal, but also constructs the view of their role as one that is part of the process rather than a consultative aspect at the start or finish of a project, as we have seen previously in large-scale renewal projects. This consultation is often delivered by a government agency as part of their broader remit. The focus on communities in the Vale of Glamorgan in terms of partnerships is also important as the rural renewal programme is so wide ranging: the large number of smaller projects in the area would seem to suggest more coordination and exercise of power from the centre, or from agencies delivering on behalf of central departments.

Partners or networks: roles, power and who governs?
Governing rural renewal in the Vale of Glamorgan

In terms of key themes, in terms of a governance and public policy perspective, one of the Vale's main achievements is to combine through governance the wide range of sectors and actors in rural renewal projects. The scope of this rural renewal initiative is far wider than its geographical focus; the means of applying such an approach in design and delivery of governance mechanisms examining the partnership approach with a central focus on the community actor and the local level in delivery and coordinating the rural renewal partnership is both innovative and intriguing, and generates substantial comparison for further similar research. Indeed, the theoretical and practical underpinnings of these projects in the Vale are major strengths and distinctive features.

That power relations and roles in the notion of partnerships are constructed and driven by the funding and resource awarding bodies

In examining the key actors in the Vale who deliver and fund the rural renewal projects, there are three levels (across two phases of funding) that are involved. The initial stages of the projects were driven by European funding, with the subsequent stages funded by the Welsh Government: the supra national and national tiers are linked through the contingencies of the funding to the local authority, who drive and coordinate the many local project areas. To be sure, there is also an important role in terms of local scrutiny and accountability in the governance of the rural renewal projects, performed by the advisory board. The main connections between these key actors – supra national, national, local and community – and connected by the stronger, bold arrowed lines in the network model in Figure 4.2. These arrows illustrate the direction of funding and coordination, which is driven by these major actors. Though there are elements

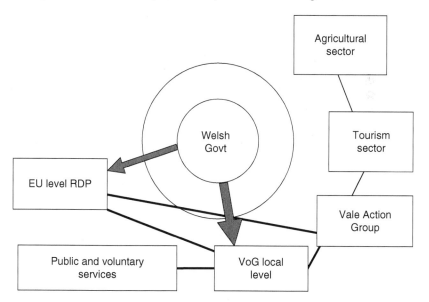

Figure 4.2 Network governance and partnership model in the Vale of Glamorgan.

here in the Vale case study of a self-organising network – particularly focused on the local authority – the funding sources show that there are broader coordinating mechanisms at the supra and national levels: after all, the Vale is one of several European rural development cases driven by this pot of funding. In each case, at the first and second phases of the rural renewal projects, there are European (first phase) and national (Welsh Government-second phase) funding criteria which evidently the rural renewal projects across the Vale must comply with, in common with any successful bidder. These processes demonstrate aspects of power between actors in the governance partnership, and also emphasise the difference in roles between actors in delivery. Though the accountability of the Advisory Board in the Vale, as discussed earlier in this chapter, does increase scrutiny and community participation in the oversight and delivery of projects, it remains essentially a product of function rather than real power, a condition of funding from the national level. Though this board is able to employ staff and consider rural renewal project proposals from the community, they work in partnership with the local level, but not with the funders at the national (and previously supra national) levels. Let us consider the question of austerity in terms of the Vale rural renewal projects. What does this tell us about roles and power in governance? The effect of cuts to local authority budgets in the UK (including devolved nations) has limited the ability of the local level to drive forward aspects of rural renewal. Despite the austerity measures and resultant cuts, several projects have seen significant outcomes and progress in the Vale, around areas such as: education, tourism, countryside and land protection, agriculture, and community groups. However, the themes of power and funding are linked. The power lies with the funding actors in governance, rather than with the local level or the advisory board or community groups. If funding is removed, it is removed by national-level actors. The direction of resource allocation and the large number of actors engaged in delivery show clear differences in role across the governance and delivery of the rural renewal projects across the Vale. Therefore, we need to consider if the governance of the projects can be described as a partnership, or for example, as a network or collaboration.

Turning to the policy networks framework, the actors are driven by multi-level tiers of governance – the supra national and, more latterly, the national centre of the Welsh Government. Though this book refers to the role of targets and outcomes, and economy, echoing NPM and its attendant emphasis on the roles and relations between intra-organisational actors operating at the agency level and at arm's length from government, which underpins the partnership and the policy networks framework, the rural renewal governance structure in the Vale also has elements of the New Public Governance approach. Though the underpinning focus of New Public Governance (NPG), as Osborne (2010) suggests, is not to determine a new regime of the discipline but rather to explore the emergence of a new typology of governance, this is driven by the endurance of aspects of NPM such as targets and measurement, the proliferation of the partnership (or network) approach to large-scale projects in governance and delivery. The collaborative approach is echoed in the rural renewal across the Vale and, despite including elements of contracting out to the private sector by the national (Welsh) Government, the influence and conditions of European level funding, and operating across several aims and outcomes the roles and relations between actors in the Vale, are clear. Though the partnership governance approach has often been crowded out by too many actors and confusion over roles and delivery, the roles in the Vale's partnership are driven clearly by three main actors. These are the Welsh Government, the Vale of Glamorgan local authority and the Vale of Glamorgan Action Group, notable for the accountability this actor brings to partnership (or network) governance arrangements (Sorensen, 2013). These actors are vital in funding, coordination and delivery. In examining the roles of these actors and their relations in the governance partnership, and turning to Bevir and Rhodes (2003, 2008) and also Marsh (2008), we see the focus on roles and interpretations across the partnership as a key aspect of the delivery of projects by the governance partnership (Shand, 2013). Bevir and Rhodes (2006) went on to argue the case for narratives, that is, stories of governance being the key explanatory tool rather than the notion of a fixed model, with the emphasis from the interpretivist perspective on actors constructions of their role and that of others. In examining governance, 'we can only tell particular stories from particular perspectives, we cannot identify a uniquely accurate model' (Bevir and Rhodes, 2008: 730). Marsh (2008) notes that while Bevir and Rhodes accept that power is structured between elites, there is not enough acknowledge in the differentiated polity narrative (as well as the DPM) that the power inequalities between actors in the policy network not only affect interpretations of each actors role, they also reflect exogenous inequalities such as their position vis-à-vis government, class, economic, and status positions. Though Bevir and Rhodes (2008) assert their governance narrative does take account of the privileged position of certain elites, Marsh (2011) suggests that the interpretivist position inevitably favours the agency of actors in the policy network to negotiate their own position (albeit within the previously noted limits). For Marsh, this view neglects the question of dialectic in governance between structure and agency.

The key decision making in this case study's network governance model is due, in the main, to the larger actors possessing more autonomy and resources, and therefore being able to achieve and prioritise targets. The most powerful actors are connected to the centre and each other by bold lines, such as the EU level, the local level and the Vale Action Group, whereas smaller actors, marginalised to some extent by the larger stakeholders, are shown in lighter lines. This reflects the hierarchy in the model. The smaller actors are illustrated as connected by the lighter lines to reflect the fact they do not control large resources, nor wield large autonomy in decision making, when compared to powerful actors such as the local level. In terms of the rural renewal projects, there has been a similar local response in the area as we see nationally in the UK, with the voluntary sector taking over or widening their brief in terms of some projects related to rural renewal and regeneration, such as working with socially excluded groups.

The bold arrows indicate the direction of flows and resources, from the key funders such as the European level and Welsh Government. This funding and the related rural renewal projects are driven by the Vale of Glamorgan local level. The local level, in driving the delivery of the rural renewal projects, works with, as we have seen, a range of public, private and voluntary sector actors across the Vale and especially in working with the Vale Action Group, which represents the community through involvement in funding awards. This visibility and accountability of the community actor in the governance and decision-making process reflects the emphasis on partnership governance and delivery across a range of actors including public, voluntary and the private sectors.

Concluding remarks

Through this discussion of the projects such as town and rural land development, the key funders in delivery and the roles and power relations between actors in the management of these renewal goals have been highlighted, in particular the role of funding from the EU, Welsh Government and the role of the community, and the important role of the local level. The governance pattern in the Vale's rural renewal has, it seems, moved toward more of a mirror image of funding. The projects and broader governance of rural renewal in the Vale of Glamorgan has, in common with the funding and project requirements set out in differing phases of the projects both from the European and national level, maintained and driven a partnership driven model, accepting the inequalities and relations in roles and power. The key actors in this model, however, do not only comprise public or voluntary sector actors. As noted above, existing local businesses and companies play a key role in projects in the Vale. The role of funders, however, reveals more about the influence of roles in governance, function and decision making in the rural renewal projects across the Vale. The importance of the roles of actors in the partnership in terms of governance is in the effect this has on the projects in rural renewal and the focus on tourism, agriculture, town and beach development and housing and job creation.

Across rural renewal projects in the Vale, the focus on these areas of development shows the vital role of the local level in delivery and in working with a range of public, private and voluntary sector actors. The community also plays a role as manager in the projects in distributing resources to each of the smaller actors. The role of communities in the Vale of Glamorgan was one driven by both European and national funding and the need to continue the model of community engagement and management of the rural renewal programme to emphasise the partnership governance aspect of the conditions and priorities of funders and in delivering across such as wide range of themes in achieving and in developing infrastructure in the short and longer term in terms of rural renewal across the Vale of Glamorgan.

Key themes in the Vale of Glamorgan

- Key role of European and Welsh Government funding
- Focus of partnership between local level and Action Group
- Key focus on expansion and development of agriculture and tourism
- Town centres, seafront and rural land development
- Need to attract and retain people in the area
- Development of existing civic infrastructure and public services and voluntary sector

5 Australia

New South Wales

This chapter examines the second empirical case. This Australian case study, New South Wales, is driven by key partnerships involving the agricultural, business, governmental and educational sectors. These are actors such as key businesses and benefactors in the region and existing agricultural practice, working towards developing existing strength and developing infrastructure, in terms of public bodies, micro level and broader community projects and enterprise. The community is a focus of several of the many rural renewal projects in the NSW region and, as such, an important partner in the governance design and delivery of rural renewal and development in the NSW region. This chapter begins with an overview of some of these key projects and the partners who are engaged in their governance, before moving on to examine the key targets in some of the projects. The chapter then examines the governance model in the region, drawing upon the policy networks approach to examine the power relations and behaviours between the actors in the partnership.

Governing rural renewal in New South Wales

In New South Wales (State/Territory) 30.9% of people were attending an educational institution. Of these, 25.7% were in primary school, 21.2% in secondary school and 22.1% in a tertiary or technical institution. There were 3,334,858 people who reported being in the labour force in the week before Census night in New South Wales (State/Territory). Of these 60.2% were employed full time, 28.2% were employed part-time and 5.9% were unemployed. The median age of people employed full-time in New South Wales (State/Territory) was 41 years and for people who were employed part-time was 40 years. The most common occupations in New South Wales (State/Territory) included Professionals 22.7%, Clerical and Administrative Workers 15.1%, Managers 13.3%, Technicians and Trades Workers 13.2%, and Community and Personal Service Workers 9.5%.

(www.abs.gov.au, 2015)

Turning to the demographic context and underpinning social statistics above, the key areas of focus in rural renewal projects are reflected in aspects of social life. The need to invest in education across the state of NSW is reflected in the statistics – 57.2% of the population has post-school educational qualifications. The overall population for the state of NSW was 6,917,656 in the 2011 Census, showing a rise of 5.6% from the 2006 Census (www.abs.gov.au, 2015). The need to connect and expand existing expertise in agriculture and develop public and civic infrastructure is driven by the rising population and the longer-term sustainability of the projects and outcomes. As will be discussed in more detail later on in this chapter, the focus and holistic approach to sustainability across the rural renewal projects in NSW involves land use, economic development and restoration of existing buildings.

Overview of key projects and partners

Rural renewal in NSW is part of the much wider context of rural renewal and development in Australia, which places emphasis on the role of communities in both the design and delivery of governance of these programmes. The role of communities embedded in the governance of rural renewal is reflected by an:

> ideology behind the discourses of rural development is one based upon notions of individual and community responsibility, self-help and 'bottom up' techniques which mobilise the skills and resources of the local community and consequently 'empower' it from the imposing structures of government programmes.
>
> (Herbert-Cheshire, 2000: 203)

To what extent the structure of large-scale rural renewal initiatives can embed the community (or related groups) in governance is a key question for the partnership. Though the community is part of this arrangement, and central to many of the aims in NSW, the extent to which it is empowered is unclear. The community certainly benefits from funding and resources, from the Foundation for Rural and Regional Renewal (FRRR) government agency, government departments and individual benefactors or businesses. However, in terms of empowerment, the community looks to be reliant on such resources and in so doing, the power of the agency, departments and other funders in the partnership is reinforced.

What is the role of communities in the rural renewal projects?

This focus on community engagement in governing and delivering rural renewal is driven, as Herbert-Cheshire notes, by the desire to ape the success of US community development programmes 'in the 1970s and 1980s' (Keane, 1990: 292, cited in Herbert-Cheshire, 2000: 203). Economic development in Australia is centred on the role of developing communities alongside developing rural land. In rural development and in large-scale rural renewal initiatives, such as the NSW case study we are concerned with here:

> It has been increasingly recognised that the task of developing rural Australia is more than simply a matter of ameliorating the problems of agriculture. Current initiatives now focus predominantly on issues of rural *community* development, incorporating strategies for the sustainability of the economic, social cultural spheres of rural life.
> (Herbert-Cheshire, 1998, cited in Herbert-Cheshire, 2000: 203)

Herbert-Cheshire draws upon the Foucauldian notion of governmentality in her discussion of Australia's rural renewal, suggesting that empowerment is not defined by the ability of the community to set and achieve goals, generate their own resource or funding, but rather by their ability to achieve empowerment through engagement with the process of governance. For Herbert-Cheshire (2000, 2004), communities can achieve this in the following way: 'Empowerment comes to be defined simply as a process which heightens an individual's capacity to act on his or her own behalf, regardless of nay structural constraints which restrict the outcome of that action' (Herbert-Cheshire, 2000: 209). However, this approach may enhance and develop self-government in individuals, but from a community or a collective action perspective this stance limits the community's broader collective ability to influence goals in rural renewal programmes, set their own targets and to win resources. In a plurality of actors – what we might term a classic partnership – resources and decision making are shared; but we see, despite the focus on the role of communities and their participation in achieving rural renewal projects, inequalities in the roles the partners have and the way in which resources are divided. The key issue of empowerment is related to setting targets, rather than being funded to achieve targets.

The role of targets in rural renewal in Australia is also underpinned by several tenets which relate to New Public Management. These underpinning themes of the importance of outputs and targets, driven by managerialism, support the case for inequalities and asymmetries in the partnership. Though community groups may be empowered in achieving such goals, or may benefit through them, the funders setting targets (particularly driven by efficiency rather than soft or less measurable goals) creates an asymmetry and a resource dependency between the partners. The focus on achieving targets is underpinned by

> Efficiency, effectiveness and competitiveness are imperatives for agricultural development. This involves the adoption of improved production

practices, up to date management and marketing technology, entrepreneurial and innovative practices which provide scope for flexibility and creativity in the diversification of the economic base.

(Gannon, 1998: 25, cited in Herbert-Cheshire, 2000: 208)

The focus on targets and outcomes is highly important in any renewal programme, whether rural or urban, large or small. However, the neo-pluralist aspect of design in the governance of these projects is illustrated by the role of who sets and funds these targets, The power relations between the actors in the partnership are exemplified by these funding and resource capacities. Turning to the work of Bevir (2003, 2008) the behavioural aspect of these inequalities in the partnership affects the behaviours and the interactions between the actors (Sullivan, 2011). For example, if one actor is setting targets in rural renewal projects, or is awarding funding as in the case of the FRRR (an example replicated across many rural and urban renewal initiatives), this influences the behaviour of smaller actors in the partnership towards ideas and solutions which fit with the requirements or priorities of the funders. Similarly, the funding once secured may then have to be diverted toward targets which the funder has prioritised. This interpretation of roles reinforces the asymmetries and differences in the governance partnership, meaning that smaller actors will become more resource dependent. The further they interpret their role in governance as being resource dependent reinforces the inequalities in the policy network, as these individuals enact institutional roles (Bevir and Rhodes, 2006, 2011) Similarly, this asymmetry between the actors then reinforces the agency, government department or businesses' role as the decision-making partner, raising the question of the suitability of the term partnership: is it a partnership, or a network? The roles and interpretation of these roles between the governance partners in rural renewal projects in NSW are set out in Figure 5.1.

Institutional context

In terms of institutional design, the key actors in driving and funding the projects are agencies driven by funds and priorities set at the national, not NSW state, level. This demonstrates the important role of the key central

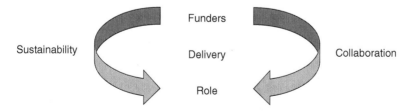

Figure 5.1 Roles and interpretations in governance networks and partnerships in New South Wales.

agencies in steering the constituent rural renewal projects to the coordinated national agenda. The priorities, funding and setting of the governance partnership – including the themes of projects which may be funded – are decisions taken at the national level, setting the context of the roles of the actors engaged in delivery of the rural renewal projects.

The governance power relations and respective roles are then ascribed by the national rather than state level, and the construction of roles and the rules of engagement within the policy network are created. The roles of the other actors in the partnership are constructed by the role of national government as the key decision maker and funder, through the role of the FRRR. The funding and coordination of the projects by the FRRR on behalf of the centre has not been crowded out or constrained by the federal structure, with the role of the agency being to drive a diverse range of projects across cities within NSW.

Who are the relevant stakeholders in the rural renewal projects?

The range of partners engaged in rural renewal in NSW is vast, and mostly represented by governmental organisations (departments and agencies), voluntary sector organisations and businesses or individual benefactors. The range of partners involved in the delivery of rural renewal reflects the sheer scale of the programme; not only because of the size of the state but due to the number of projects being undertaken in the region. The list of partners is set out in Table 5.1, grouped by sector and founding partners. This range of actors engaged in both the design and delivery of rural renewal projects in NSW reflects the key aspects of these initiatives and the range of partners both in terms of sector and size, such as government departments, agencies, private sector organisations and individual benefactors, working with rural communities, related groups and voluntary sector organisations. It is key that the FRRR list set out in Table 5.1 separates the foundations and individual donors from the partners. This illustrates the importance of the FRRR in two ways in governing rural renewal. First, its role in working with such benefactors; and, second, in coordinating and funding the partners in delivery of the projects.

The key focuses of ecology, development of communities and resource management all demonstrate the underpinning values of sustainability in the NSW rural renewal projects. These are overarching and anchored in both short and longer-term goals:

> Following the emergence of a nascent new social movement's politics in the 1960s, however, the environment became a greater influence in mainstream politics. By the 1980s, discussions were emerging on the international stage around the problem of incorporating sustainable development strategies into the domestic policy on environment protection. In the UK, despite several positive reactions to international

summits and agendas – notably Rio in 1987, Kyoto in 1997 and Johannesburg in 2002, the problem of implementing sustainable development practices on the ground was still proving difficult. Agenda 21, as noted in Chapter 2, was a domestic transfusion of the WCEDs original rallying cry to 'think global, act local' (WCED, 1987) in '*Our Common Future*'; but was ill suited to the regulatory, unitary pattern of UK government. The development of government networks to try to achieve a best-fit mediation of stakeholder interests was similarly ill contrived, as Munton (Munton, 1997: 150) observes, that 'what distinguishes the new context from the more familiar arena of land-use conflict is a set of political commitments to "sustainable development" which may prove difficult to abandon when their more uncomfortable implications become clear'.

(Shand, 2013: 33)

The differentiated polity and the focus on both short and longer-term targets shows the lasting effect of NPM and the partnership focus emphasises the approach of the New Public Governance paradigm, and this approach of the network and/or partnership model of governance delivery is widespread in renewal programmes. In the NSW rural renewal projects there are several examples of micro level or individual projects which are funded by individual benefactors or by the FRRR. Some examples of such projects are set out in the sections below, demonstrating the breadth of funders in rural renewal and the community focus of the projects, as discussed in the earlier sections of this chapter. The examples of projects set out below are illustrative of the micro focus of some of the funding from the FRRR, and also the role of the Rural Education Programme (REP), which is additionally set up and funded by the FRRR. The REP works with schools and communities in rural areas in funding educational and socially sustainable programmes relating to local flora, fauna and environmental or broader community initiatives.

The Rural Education Programme (REP) and the FRRR

The FRRR has developed the Rural Education Programme (REP) to further integrate the funding of projects by the government agency and by individual private benefactors. The role of the REP is in widening participation and access to education from rural communities and for student cohorts which typically have a high percentage of first attenders at university or non-traditional achiever students. Rural renewal projects funded by the REP typically tend to address questions or themes such as, how can the community support students coming through non-traditional routes rather than the 'traditional' route in education; what can funders do to bring down the barriers rural communities experience in access and in the traditional route, and if they still exist. The examples below detail the work of the REP in terms of embedding these questions in the rural

Table 5.1 Partners engaged in governance and delivery of rural renewal programmes in NSW

Founding members	Donors	Partnerships	Individual donations ($5,000 and above)
Commonwealth Government of Australia	Alf & Meg Steel Fund	ACER/Tender Bridge	Neilma Gantner
Sidney Myer Fund	ANZ Banking Group	Australia Post	Alexandra Gartmann
	ANZ Trustees, who administer:	ABC Heywire	Lady Southey
	The McEwen Foundation	Australian Community Philanthropy	Noel Weaver
	The William Buckland Foundation	Australian Environmental Grantmakers	
	The Sylvia & Charles Viertel Charitable Trust	Network	
	The Robert William Robertson Estate	Desert Knowledge Australia	
	Aurizon Community Giving Fund	Herbert Smith Freehills	
	Aussie Farmers Foundation	Philanthropy Australia	
	Australian Community Foundation	Regional Australia Institute	
	Bertalli Family Foundation	The Pratt Foundation	
	Betty Fulton Fund	Perpetual Trustees, who administer:	
	The Carbine Club	The Berrembed Trust	
	Davies Family Foundation	The Estate of the Late Harold Gordon Jones	
	Department of Family and Community Services (FACS) NSW	The H & L Hecht Trust	
	Department of Infrastructure and Regional Development	The Julian Flett Endowment	
		The Ledger Charitable Trust	
	Department of State Development, Business and Innovation VIC	The Margaret Lawrence Bequest	
		The Percy Baxter Charitable Trust	
	Deutsche Bank	The SBA Foundation	
	Doc Ross Family Foundation	Portland House Group	
		Price Family Foundation	

The Estate of the Late Edward Wilson
The Gardiner Foundation
Geoff & Helen Handbury Foundation
The Ian Potter Foundation
The John & Janet Calvert-Jones Foundation
John T Reid Charitable Trusts
The Maple-Brown Family Foundation
McCusker Charitable Foundation
The Myer Family Company
The Myer Foundation
Origin Foundation

The QBE Foundation
Queensland Community Foundation
The Rali Foundation
Queensland Community Foundation
The Rali Foundation
The R.E. Ross Trust
The Rees Family Foundation
School Aid Trust
Sid & Fiona Myer Family Foundation
Sidney Myer Fund
Stan and Maureen Duke Foundation
Suncorp
State Trustees, who administer:
– The John Sylvester Feehan Charitable Trust
– William Austin Zeal Charitable Trust
– William Henry Hutchinson Charitable Trust
Target
Thyne Reid Foundation
Third Link
Tim Fairfax Family Foundation
The Trust Company
Victorian Bushfire Appeal Fund
Vincent Fairfax Family Foundation
VISY Employee Community Fund
Wilson HTM
The Yulgilbar Foundation

Source: FRRR, 2010.

renewal initiatives in NSW, and are also a means of placing longer-term social and economic sustainability in the area, through higher access, attainment and engagement for rural families in education. These roles in the context of sustainability are examined in more detail in later sections, but first let us turn to a summary of grants awarded by the REP to rural communities in supporting education.

> The establishment of the Rural Education Program (REP) meant for FRRR an opportunity early in the life of the Foundation to work with a committed and passionate group of private donors to further an important aspect of the foundation's responsibilities – educational disadvantage. The work of REP was highly complementary to other FRRR programs such as the Back to School Program, E3 Grants program with the RASF NSW and Australia Posts' Stretching the Envelope Small Grants Program and the REACH – Rural Early Childhood Grants Program. REP was the first FRRR program to highlight the importance of access to good educational opportunities for school students in rural and remote Australia. The REP program will be greatly missed because of the niche funding provided in grants that truly reached many remote and disadvantaged communities and helped expand educational horizons.
>
> (FRRR REP Report, 2010)

The use of fire in land restoration and rural renewal in NSW: partnerships and governance

Other examples of sustainable renewal in NSW focus on land restoration and fire. The aim of using fire in land restoration is to ensure biodiversity and sustainability. The arrangements for delivery of these projects are also driven by partnerships. Though there is less of a plurality of actors in these partnership arrangements, primarily due to the small range of actors engaged in governance and delivery, there are also clear power relations driven by roles, as we can see from which actors hold power and which hold function. First, the role of funding: the actors in these project areas who deliver funding, such as the National Parks and Wildlife Service, Crown Lands and the NSW Rural Fire Service, show clear power structures. In addition, the fire restoration projects link these larger actors with smaller, more micro level, actors such as the Yarrawarra Aboriginal Corporation. The leadership and coordination between these actors is driven by the goal of partnership. Rather than a network, as there are so few large actors in these projects, the delivery of projects is more easily led and coordinated, and therefore there is far less risk of miscommunication or competing targets or goals between the partners jeopardising or frustrating delivery or management of the projects. Evidently, this is more urgent in the governance of aspects of rural renewal (in NSW and elsewhere) which draw upon techniques such as fire use in land management and this is an engaging example of larger funding actors from local and state tiers of governance working directly with communities in their land.

> Temperate native grasslands and grassy woodlands are among Australia's most endangered ecological communities. In recent years Greening Australia's Victorian-based Grassy Groundcover Restoration program demonstrated the efficacy of complex herbaceous restoration on ex-agricultural lands by direct seeding. Following site establishment the program focussed on the management of biomass to preserve diversity and manage fuel loads. Fire and other techniques were repeatedly tested. This presentation will discuss the use of fire as a management tool in restored and remnant grasslands and grassy woodlands. It will explore how and why fire is useful in these systems, but also some of the constraints around its application. There will also be discussion of alternative or complimentary approaches. Examples will illustrate reconstructed grassy-type communities, and the use of fire and other biomass management techniques.
>
> (Nature Conservation Council, 2015)

The role of partnerships in land management with fire is evidenced here by the design and delivery of governance: the key partners set out above are the Endangered Ecological Communities (EECs), the Yarrawarra Bush Regeneration Team and members of the Aboriginal community, and the NSW RFS. This example of rural regeneration is interesting in terms of partnerships, as it is a small number of partners overseeing and delivering a dangerous aspect of land management over a wide geographic area. In this example of rural renewal, coordination and clear targets are obviously vital in ensuring the safety of these partners and the practice of fire land management. Interestingly, the role of communities is embedded in this practice – the underpinning aim of engaging communities in the design and delivery of rural renewal in NSW (and as we have seen earlier in this chapter, in rural renewal in Australia more broadly) is present in projects which are both ecologically and socially based.

> The Cultural, Burning & Bush Regeneration in Garby Country Project brought together key partners including Yarrawarra Aboriginal Corporation, National Parks & Wildlife Service, Crown Lands and the NSW Rural Fire Service. The project aimed to develop and implement an integrated and culturally appropriate program of prescribed burning and bush regeneration at priority coastal lowland and headlands sites within the traditional lands of the Garby People of the Gumbaynggirr Nation. The Garby Elders are traditional custodians of the north-east lowland Gumbanyggirr Country, responsible for the protection and maintenance of Cultural Sites under traditional lore.

The project sites contain Aboriginal heritage assets and culturally important resources, food and medicines and include Endangered Ecological Communities (EECs) and habitat for threatened species. The activities conducted through the project included integrated bush regeneration and prescribed burning programs aiming to improve the ecological and cultural condition and resilience of these culturally important sites. Working with members of the Yarrawarra Bush Regeneration Team and other interested members of the Aboriginal community the NSW RFS provided recognised competency-based fire training and capacity building opportunities and facilitated community participation in on-ground fire operations.

(Nature Conservation Council, 2015)

More community level focus is also evident in projects which provide facilities for the community to use, such as renovating derelict or abandoned buildings. This reflects some renewal successes in Australia which, as mentioned in Chapter 2, have drawn upon a combination of Greenfield, brownfield and greyfield renewal programmes. In terms of these aspects of rural renewal, there are brownfield aspects in terms of restoration of buildings, but also greenfield examples in terms of ecology, land and flora and fauna. Both of these rural renewal examples also emphasise the social and environmental aspects of sustainability in terms of heritage and renovation of disused buildings, which are discussed in more length in the following sections.

Using heritage for rural renewal in NSW: partnerships and governance

Examples of heritage, particularly in the use of buildings, illustrate the underpinning role of communities in the rural renewal programmes. These communities, additionally, are couched in the idea of governance partnerships, working with the Heritage Council and heritage and conservation groups in restoring buildings for future use.

Rural and urban communities are becoming much more sophisticated in using their heritage to enhance the appeal of their towns and neighbourhoods. One of the key ways they are doing this is by giving their heritage buildings and precincts a new lease of life through adaptation.

These communities are seizing the opportunity to extend the life of their heritage items by making them useful – by giving them new and productive purposes. Through innovation they are achieving the twin goals of heritage conservation and financial viability. The Heritage Council travels all over the State to meet people who are passionate about heritage and to see what they have done to showcase their local heritage places. Because of the concentration of human and financial resources in the cities we expect to find good examples of adaptive reuse in the major population centres. It is therefore particularly satisfying that, as well as showcasing some excellent examples from metropolitan areas, this publication also demonstrates how well some regional and rural communities do this kind of work, given the greater challenges they face in terms of funding and resources. This publication includes case studies demonstrating best practice in both the rural and the urban context. There are many other examples around the state of local heritage items that have been successfully adapted for cafés and restaurants. The Heritage Council was delighted to be involved in this publication, particularly since it highlights such a variety of remarkable projects.

(FRRR Community Report, 2007)

These examples in rural renewal in NSW show several aspects of sustainability, both in terms of biodiversity and land use, but also in terms of embedding governance structures. First, let us take the notion of governance and sustainable communities. The underpinning aim of community engagement in the rural renewal initiatives is illustrated well by the role of community in governance in terms of design and delivery. As noted in terms of rural and urban development, this is a vital underpinning theme:

The term sustainable development has evolved from its first widespread usage in the World Commission on Environmental Developments (WCED) *'Our Common Future'* (1987), where it was defined as 'development that meets the needs of the present without compromising the ability of future generations to meet their own needs' (WCED, 1987). As Mebratu notes, this report constituted a 'major turning point for the concept of sustainable development' (1998: 496). Mebratu observes that the evolution of the term's usage has undergone a staged process of change. That *'Our Common Future'* was 'neither the starting point nor the possible end of the conceptual development process' (1998: 496). Mebratu sets out three phases of usage. (i) Pre-Stockholm (–1972); (ii) Stockholm to WCED (1972–1987); (iii) Post WCED (1987–1997). As Rydin has noted, sustainability has been loosely applied to the urban renewal process. The question of what constitutes 'sustainable development' in the planning project has been modelled by O'Riordan *et al.* (2001) as composed of The Three Pillars; the economic, social and environmental. O'Riordan has also described the Russian Doll model, in which the three spheres are ranked in order of importance, with the economic at the centre. Both models demonstrate the flexibility of the term sustainable development and the failure to define what constitutes 'sustainability'.

(Shand, 2013)

Moreover, in fostering sustainable communities, these structures ensure the development and legacy of community involvement in the governance and delivery of rural renewal.

Second, the role of sustainable land use. Both the examples above of fire usage and of heritage buildings emphasise sustainability in terms of ecology and social spheres. The use of fire in rural development is designed, as we have seen above, to facilitate management of different grasses and plant life in a sustainable manner, to provide biodiversity.

Third, the example of heritage and use of buildings (often for several different uses than these buildings were originally employed) brings together different strands of sustainability; the environmental and the social. Renovating previously used buildings for new uses is both an obvious environmental mechanism – in place of building newer units with the potential to increase emissions and pollution – but also feeds into the social aspect of sustainability, as the conversion creates public good through the renovation and the eventual uses of the building by the community and local groups. The linkage between these aspects of sustainability, which itself remains such a contested term in both its underpinning theory and in its practical application, provides a more holistic dynamic to the rural renewal programmes in NSW. The linkage between physical land, flora and fauna and the community is integral to achieving success, both short and longer term, in the rural renewal programmes. The connectedness of the community to the land through business, governance, and public and community life is central to developing both projects and targets, and the example particularly of using heritage buildings for new and innovative uses is a core aspect of the sustainability in delivery of the rural renewal projects.

Heritage conservation can be a catalyst for improving social, economic and environmental outcomes when urban areas in towns and cities are being regenerated. Heritage items create a sense of place – they have local character and identity – and communities feel strongly about what happens to them. Large-scale adaptation projects, or heritage-led regeneration projects, account for some of this state's most successful urban, regional and rural regeneration projects by renewing the economic, social and environmental vitality of local areas in decline. The key to heritage-led regeneration is understanding the heritage significance of the place, and how the different features of the site contribute to its significance. The historic environment can encompass landscape, townscape, archaeological, built and Aboriginal heritage values. Specialist knowledge can contribute to the success of heritage-led regeneration projects at every stage: during the initial planning and assessment, master or concept planning stages; and the construction and completion phases of the project. The potential to conserve, provide long-term sustainable uses, and interpret the heritage values of the place can be integrated into the project, thereby increasing the potential for long-term benefits. Engaging appropriate professional advice from the outset, and consulting the local council (and in the case of State heritage significant sites, the Heritage Council of NSW) early will help develop a common understanding about what is considered appropriate. Engaging with the local community early in the project will avoid resistance to the project at a later stage and can provide fruitful local support and partnerships, as well as contribute vital information to the interpretation of the place.

(FRRR REP Report, 2010)

Though sustainability and sustainable development, as we have seen, remain highly contested terms, the rural renewal projects in NSW combine resource efficiency – such as the brownfield themes of reuse of buildings discussed above – with the social emphasis we have witnessed in the heritage projects. As we have seen in areas of the (vast) sustainability literature, the discussions triple bottom line or three pillars have been argued to have evolved to the triple crunch. The triple crunch focuses on the scarcity of resources, government austerity and food. These ideas are worth contemplating in terms of the NSW rural renewal programmes: the suitable use of resources, integrated with use of existing infrastructure such as communal buildings and the development (and participation) of communities embedded within the projects.

As Davies (2002) observes, these 'partnerships' constitute a distinct mode of governance. Following Davies, it is possible to problematise these partnerships and networks; that 'the state is still more than capable of getting its way in the politics of urban renewal' (Davies, 2002: 302), by the ownership of resources, (conceptualised as the Asymmetric Power Model by Marsh *et al.*, 2003). Governance is a key theme of the research questions and the roles and relations across the partnership approach in which the governance model is controlled by key actors who drive projects, funding and targets:

This move from the traditional historic-legal unitary Westminster model of British government to the governance model, first captured by Rhodes (1997) as the DPM of agencies hollowed out from the centre, has been critiqued by – among others, but most relevantly here – Marsh, Richards and Smith (2003) in their APM. The APM concedes that the disaggregating process of the DPM has taken place, but suggests that rather than merely the business of government being hollowed out to these spheres of governance via territory and function, the centre (government) still holds sway via the means of controlling the distribution of resources. The hollowing out effect in UK governance has been brought about by the rise of QUANGOs in the business of governing. These functional bodies carry out the business of aspects of government. These agencies have impacted on the notion of regulation in UK governance, as they are responsible ultimately to the centre, and despite enjoying a large functional responsibility, can be reined in by the centre.

(Shand, 2013: 12–13)

Table 5.2 Outcomes and funding of projects in New South Wales

Project/aim	Time period	Funder(s)	Cost ($)	Outcome
Building Community Through Technology (Queensland) Condamine State School Parents and Citizens Association ANZ Seeds of Renewal Program		FRRR	6,000	
Boosting the Social Heart of a Small Town		FRRR	3,000	
Painting a Town's Story (Queensland)		FRRR	6,000	
Raising Awareness of the Dangers of Litter through Art (South Australia) Kangaroo Island Community Education		FRRR	5,000	
Rural Education Program Grants 2004–2006	2004–2006	FRRR		
Organisation Project State Grant				
Arts Outwest Inc Forbes Parkes Lachlan Small Schools NSW Literacy Project				
Baimbridge College Standing Tall VIC			6,000	
Bairnsdale Secondary College Specialist Digital English Classroom VIC			3,000	
Bairnsdale Secondary College Evaluation of Specialist Digital English Classroom VIC			6,000	
Balmoral High School Music Equipment VIC			5,000	
Barmah Kindergarten & Occasional Library VIC			6,000	
Child Care Inc			25,000	
Berry Street Victoria Seymour Community Based VCAL VIC			23,000	
Blackthorn College P & F Association Tiered Seating QLD			1,900	
Bollon District Childrens Resident Comm Upgrade Computer, Purchase Freezer & Dryer QLD 4,247			7,500	
Boort Secondary College Instrumental Music Program VIC 21,880			4,515	
Branxholme – Wallacedale Comm School Cultural Excursion Melbourne VIC 3,000			9,470	
Bright Adult Education Inc. Words on Wheels: Adult Literacy			4,000	

Burnett Head State School P & C Assoc. Going Green QLD	4,000
Cairns School of Distance Education Skilling Home Tutors QLD	1,000
Cairns School of Distance Education Cyclone Monica QLD	5,900
Carnarvon School of the Air (CSOTA) Canberra Camp 2005 WA	15,000
Centacare Wilcannia – Forbes CGEA – for Narromine Youth NSW	4,000
Charles Sturt University Research Project: Impact of Drought on NSW	20,000
Secondary Education Access in Rural & Remote Areas	90,909
Charleville & District Community Kids in Biz QLD	1,636
Support Association	9,000
Charleville School of Distance Ed P & C Accommodation for Home Tutors QLD 9,000	5,000
Development Training	8,000
Charlton & District Preschool Central Deborah Gold Mine Trip VIC 805	5,000
Charlton College Instrumental Music VIC	5,000
CHILD – The Association for Childhood Operation – TALK (Talking & Learning for	30,000
Kids) QLD	
Language & Related Disorders	24,200
Circular Head Rural Health Services Inc HIPPY – Home Interaction Program for TAS	4,00
Parents and Youngsters	
Cleve Area School Improved Facilities for Distance Education SA	
Contact Incorporated 2006 School Packs NSW	
Contact Incorporated Expanded School Packs Program 2006 NSW	
Coolgardie Primary School Bushfood Garden WA	
Coolgardie Primary School Breakfast Club	

Source: FRRR, 2015.

Who drives funding and delivery in the rural renewal projects? Rural renewal in New South Wales: projects, funding and progress

The focus on funding and delivery of rural renewal projects across NSW is, as represented in Figure 5.2, driven by the FRRR. The focus on these projects is divided across several categories for priority, such as ecological and environmental projects, public and civic projects focused around aspects like social care, education and healthcare.

> In Condamine, the Country Women's Association branch, the school, rugby club, local computer classes and the community's Melbourne Cup day function all share one thing in common: they all rely on the school's data projector and laptop computer for learning and for fun. The school used an FRRR grant to buy the equipment. Kids used it to learn how to create groovy multi-media presentations. Community groups used it to run workshops on how to use computers, the Internet and e-mail. And soon the Parents and Citizens Association began to hire it out to community groups for presentation days, social gatherings and fundraising ventures. Now the projector is the centrepiece at gatherings of the local rugby club (they love watching the finals on the big screen), the Isolated Children's Parents Association and the local CWA which uses it for their International Banquet and the community's Melbourne Cup gathering. Such events strengthen community ties, the CWA says.
>
> (FRRR REP Report, 2010)

The central role of the FRRR in funding and coordinating the rural renewal partnership shows the steering role of the agency. Though there are government departments engaged in the governance design of the rural renewal programmes, the FRRR is functionally there to deliver the projects, demonstrating a neo-pluralist approach. This asymmetry in the governance partnership shows the FRRR as coordinating the delivery of projects and funding; though they are carrying out this function on behalf of government, at arm's length as it were, the power rests with the government departments as they could theoretically take the function back from or away from the FRRR. However, there is, following the policy networks approach, a degree of disaggregation in the NSW case study as the partnership is driven by the agency and led by the agency on behalf of government. The funding and resources of the projects by the FRRR also illustrate the differences between roles of actors in the partnership, and additionally show the coordination undertaken by the agency while the leadership is undertaken by the government departments. However, the role of funding in these projects is also driven by several individual benefactors to individual projects or events and also by some private sector organisations.

FRRR projects were overwhelmingly rated as successful across all programs. A key determinant of project success was whether funding support was received from the FRRR. As part of the survey recipients were asked to rate whether the project was successful on a scale of 1 to 10 from 'not successful (1)' to 'very successful (10)'. Recipients were also asked to rate whether the project proceeded as planned on a scale of 1 to 10 from 'not at all (1)' through to 'exactly as planned (10)'. Projects that were very successful were far more likely to have proceeded exactly as planned and vice versa. The importance of FRRR providing resources to organisations who might not otherwise receive them is shown in Figure 3. The left hand panel shows that for successful applicants, the project generally proceeded as planned, and was successful. By contrast, for most unsuccessful applicants (right hand panel) the project did not go ahead as planned and, where this occurred, the project was less likely to be successful. The inference from these results is that an FRRR grant was often pivotal to projects occurring and to a successful outcome being achieved.

(FRRR REP Report, 2010)

Partners or networks: roles, power and who governs?

The key decision making in the NSW partnership governance model (Figure 5.2) is due, in the main, to the larger actors delivering the funding and resources, and therefore being able to set priorities in terms of projects

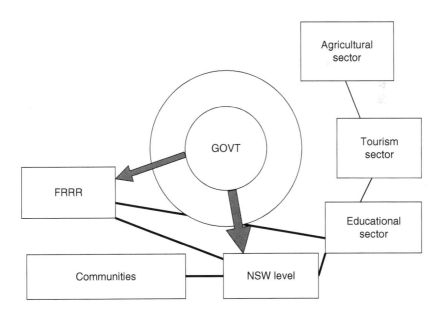

Figure 5.2 Network governance and partnership model in New South Wales.

and focus, and to fund, achieve and prioritise targets. The most powerful actors are connected to the centre and each other by bold lines, most typically the FRRR, national and state level government, whereas smaller actors, dependent on decision making and funds awarded by the larger stakeholders, are shown in lighter lines. These are also key elements in the construction of roles and the effect on power relations in the governance partnership. These differences in role between actors reflect the hierarchy in the partnership model set out above. The smaller actors are illustrated as connected by the lighter lines to reflect the fact they do not control large resources, nor wield large autonomy in decision making, when compared to powerful actors, most particularly the FRRR. In terms of delivery, there has been a broad focus across the state of NSW, taking in civic and community projects, public services, enterprise and the voluntary sector related to rural renewal, such as working with socially excluded groups.

That power relations and roles in the notion of partnerships are constructed and driven by the funding and resource awarding bodies

The role of networks and partnerships in NSW shows that the governance model is premised on partnerships of a small and powerful set of actors, driven by the FRRR in terms of project priority areas and through funding. This focus on the priority themes of projects is an important one as it constructs the roles of the various actors, and suggests the roles and power relations between the partnership actors. The key partners and set of actors in delivery and funding of the rural renewal projects are the FRRR, delivering on behalf of national government; but there are also key actors in collaboration with the FRRR, such as the national and state levels. The role of the smaller actors in the delivery of the projects shows a myriad of partners, through public sector organisations such as schools, voluntary sector bodies and charities, and small businesses. In drawing upon the theory to examine the roles and relations across the governance partnership, the power relations focus more towards the APM rather than the DPM, and in these inequalities in power relations we see the key roles driven by nationally set priorities around rural renewal and development. The delivery of these priorities reinforces the asymmetry across the governance arrangements.

Drawing on Bevir (2010) the roles of these actors are driven by power and territory (in this case, the power to determine and identify the priorities of rural renewal projects and the existing role and scope of governance). The notions of power and resistance Bevir (2004) discusses in the roles, interpretations and enactments of governance in partnerships or networks. The collaboration and delivery in rural renewal does not suggest a tension of power and resistance across collaborating actors in the projects, but rather a shared interpretation and understanding of roles. The notion of storytelling (Bevir, 2011; Sorensen, 2013) cannot be applied here as there is not a tension around role construction or strategies in delivery – rather, the shared construction of roles shows the asymmetries across governance. However, this is an important note on the interpretations of actors – do they, for example, see themselves as partners? The model (as indeed this book) makes some assumptions about notions of partnership; however, typically major actors in governance and delivery of rural renewal set out discourses of partnership, and this has been a common approach to renewal programmes, as noted in Chapter 2.

Rural renewal in New South Wales: projects, funding and progress

The focus on funding and delivery of rural renewal projects across NSW is, as represented in Figure 5.2, driven by the FRRR. The focus on these projects is divided across several categories for priority, such as ecological and environmental projects, public and civic projects focused around aspects like social care, education and healthcare:

> Over the past ten years, the FRRR has maintained a spread of grants across the main sectors of community activity in rural and regional Australia. The FRRR awards grants in six categories: Education; Social; Economic; Health; Environment; and Culture. All six categories have received at least $2 million in grants over the past ten years from the FRRR. A high proportion of recipients that applied for FRRR grants, have not previously received support from any other philanthropic organisation, or public sources of funding. Out of the survey recipients, over 75% of recipients of FRRR grants had not applied for grants from either government or other philanthropic organisations. Increasingly, it appears that smaller, largely volunteer based community groups are more able to access funding for small projects via programs operated by the FRRR than other sources. The FRRR provides services (both grants and capacity building) to a wide range of geographic areas, sectoral categories and recipient types across Australia. The FRRR's reach is evidenced by: Wide geographic reach, which appears to be extending over time. The maintenance of a spread of funding across the major categories of community activity in rural and regional Australia. The FRRR having reached many individuals and community organisations who had not received any alternative support from government or other philanthropic organisations. Basic measures of geographic spread indicate that a large and increasing number of communities have received FRRR assistance. Figure 6 shows that the number of unique postcodes receiving grants from the FRRR each year has grown substantially since 2000. Almost 500 unique postcodes received FRRR grants in 2009.
>
> (FRRR REP Report, 2010)

Concluding remarks: New South Wales rural renewal initiative

In NSW, there is a myriad of rural renewal and rural development projects, in common with several other states and territories. The wide ranging rural renewal projects across NSW have focuses such as agriculture and tourism, but also a larger focus on the support of community projects and initiatives. Public services projects are targeted, notably the educational programme driven by the FRRR. The role of the FRRR, as discussed extensively in this chapter, is the key actor in driving and funding projects across the NSW rural renewal agenda.

The focus on the wide range of funding from the FRRR across a diverse scope of projects reflects the size of the NSW state, and the need not only to develop existing infrastructure and business but also to invest in these aspects of provision. The projects section above examines the funding and key actors engaged in the governance and delivery of rural renewal projects, but across each of these, we see the central delivery role of the FRRR and the coordination of other actors through funding and key priorities.

The focus on key themes such as ecology, land use and the important role of heritage and land use demonstrate the environmental and sustainability focus of rural renewal and development across NSW. The use of derelict buildings and the transformation of these facilities into civic or community spaces, together with the focus on restoration and sustainable land use, demonstrates the emphasis on establishing and developing the NSW state's rural development as linked to the social and economic developments.

The focus on resource use reflects the triple crunch across debates in sustainability. The broad range of rural renewal projects also reflects the multi-dimensionality of sustainability, while the social aspects of community and public sector development are represented in the focus on healthcare and education, particularly the Rural Education Program of the FRRR. The funding and focus of these projects also emphasise the need to develop infrastructure and support businesses across NSW, focused on both the short and longer-term outcomes of the rural renewal projects.

Key themes in NSW

*   Sustainable development and land use
*   Focus on education and community projects
*   Funding and coordinating role of FRRR

6 South Africa
Eastern Cape

This chapter examines the third empirical case. This South African case study, the Eastern Cape, is driven by key partnerships involving the agricultural, business, governmental and educational sectors: universities in the region and existing businesses, working towards tourism and building public institutions, and capacity building public life in governance more broadly. The chapter begins by setting out the context to rural renewal in the Eastern Cape, examining the social drivers in the region and how these are linked to the key themes in rural renewal programmes, before moving on to engage with the research questions set out in Chapter 3. The chapter then sets out the aims of the projects and the main actors engaged in the design and delivery of these, focused on budgets and resources, targets and the relations across the partnership between the key actors.

This chapter examines and applies the policy networks approach and models to the rural renewal projects in the Eastern Cape, focusing on Nkonkobe and Alice. Within the case study areas, the chapter examines the role of key governance actors in funding and delivering the rural renewal projects, the role of communities and the progress of projects. The chapter goes on to examine the governance partnership model which draws upon the policy networks framework of interpretivism (Bevir, 2009; Bevir and Rhodes, 2003, 2006, 2008; Bevir and Richards, 2009a, 2009b) and using the New Public Management (NPM) and New Public Governance (NPG) approaches (Osborne, 2006, 2010), which underpin the theoretical discussion of governance in this case study chapter. The chapter examines the widespread transition from NPM to NPG, centred on the use of partnerships and networks in the governance (design and delivery) of rural renewal, regeneration, development and community engagement programmes, though within these programmes key tenets of the policy networks framework – such as the roles and power relations between actors in the governance partnership and the resultant rules of the game (that is, the power relations in the network or partnership, which come about through role construction and interpretation between the organisations involved) – are examined.

Rural renewal across the Eastern Cape

Statistics produced in 2014 by the Province of the Eastern Cape, drawing upon the 2011 census and other data, give an overview of several areas of demography in the region, which underpin the rural renewal projects across the Eastern Cape. In terms of population change and growth the data suggests the area to be a densely populated area which is experiencing growth, necessitating the development of goods, services and infrastructure:

> According to the 2011 census, the province is a home to 6.7 million people. This is equivalent to 12.7% of the national population. This makes the Eastern Cape the third most populated province after Gauteng, with a population of 12.2 million and 23.7% of the national population; and KwaZulu-Natal, with a population of 10.2 million and 19.8% of the national population. Compared with the 2001 census, the province grew by 4.5%. It shows that the 0–4 and 15–19 age cohorts are the biggest contributors to the province's population. Those under the age of 30, account for 57% of the province's population. The median ages of the province's population is 22.4 years, lower than the national median age of 24.4 years, which makes it the second youngest provincial population in South Africa. Limpopo however tops the list with a median age of 21.3 years. The relatively wealthier provinces such as the Western Cape and Gauteng occupy the last two spots in the ranking of ages with median ages of 27 and 28.6 years respectively.
>
> (www.dedea.gov.za, 2013)

Equally, the issue of age among the population of the Eastern Cape is also linked to employability and flight. Though the younger population makes up the majority of the population, there is a large problem in retaining younger people in the region through the lack of desirable employment opportunities – this is a pressing problem both in terms of keeping younger talented residents in the Eastern Cape and in attracting talented people to the area. This issue also highlights the problems, both short and longer term, in developing infrastructure and civic institutions, community groups and private sector start-ups and enterprise. In terms of gender, there is a similarly pressing problem in the region:

Table 6.1 Socio-economic data for the Eastern Cape, 2014

Eastern Cape (all EC wide stats.)	2000	2014
Population	8,009	8,749–9,443
No. of residents with no formal academic qualifications	86%	86%

The male population is marginally greater than that of the female population in the first four age cohorts. This comprises the ages between 0–4, 5–9, 10–14, and 15–19. If all the age cohorts before the age of 20 are put together, males outnumber females by a mere 1.03%. This is not however true for age cohorts above 15 to 19. In these age cohorts, the female population is noticeably larger than the male population. The bias towards females in the province's working age population alluded to above could be attributed, among others, to migration of males to wealthier provinces in search of better opportunities. The Eastern Cape is ranked number one in terms if the extent of net migration; close to 214,815 people migrated to other provinces from the Eastern Cape Province alone between 2006 and 2011.

(www.dedea.gov.za, 2013)

In terms of age in the Eastern Cape, the problems highlighted in the sections above crystallise to form a picture of a population that is ageing and in need of enhanced employability to retain talented younger people in the region. This need obviously stretches across the education, training and employability spheres, demanding the development of public and private organisations to employ and be developed by talented residents and those who could be attracted to the Eastern Cape.

The proportion of the population within the age group of 0–14 is falling while that of 15–64 is increasing and those over the age of 64 have remained more or less unchanged. The increase in the working age population (i.e. aged 15–64) may be good news when viewed from the perspective of an increased workforce. However, given the high levels of unemployment in South Africa, the potential of the workforce is already underutilized. This implies a greater challenge to the province to match a growing workforce with growing job opportunities as well as greater capacity in municipal service delivery. The 0–4 and 15–19 age cohorts are the biggest contributors to the province's population. Those under the age of 30, account for 57% of the province's population. The median ages of the province's population is 22.4 years, lower than the national median age of 24.4 years, which makes it the second youngest provincial population in South Africa. The male population is marginally greater than that of the female population in the first four age cohorts. This comprises the ages between 0–4, 5–9, 10–14, and 15–19. If all the age cohorts before the age of 20 are put together, males outnumber females by a mere 1.03%. This is not however true for age cohorts above 15 to 19. In these age cohorts, the female population is noticeably larger than the male population. The bias towards females in the province's working age population alluded to above could be attributed, among others, to migration of males to wealthier provinces in search of better opportunities. The Eastern Cape is ranked number one in terms if the extent of net migration; close to 214,815 people migrated to other provinces from the Eastern Cape Province alone between 2006 and 2011.

(www.dedea.gov.za, 2013)

The rural renewal initiative, and the projects within it, across the Eastern Cape is driven by the types of issues discussed above in the demographic makeup of the area. In addition to the problems presented by the need to provide infrastructure, employability opportunities and greater educational facilities and resources, so the area also requires development of both civic, community, educational, transport and business expertise to accommodate the expanding population in the Eastern Cape:

> Demographic statistics are crucial to direct policies that affect socio-economic conditions of the province. According to the 2011 census, the province is a home to 6.7 million people. This is equivalent to 12.7% of the national population. This makes the Eastern Cape the third most populated province after Gauteng, with a population of 12.2 million and 23.7% of the national population; and KwaZulu-Natal, with a population of 10.2 million and 19.8% of the national population. Compared with the 2001 census, the province grew by 4.5%.
>
> (www.dedea.gov.za, 2013)

The statistics discussed in the sections above set the context for rural renewal in the area, in terms of the need to grow employment in the region, encourage business development and to increase the scope for educational opportunities and attainment, working with the further and higher education providers in the area as part of the Alice regeneration strategy. The data above, drawn from the census, is based on the Nkonkobe area. The population shows some growth over the recent period, though the most recent figures are uncertain, due to the growth of the University of Fort Hare's fluctuating (and growing) population. The low number of people attending education routes, and the subsequent low number of those who leave having achieved a formal qualification, necessitates the themes of expanding educational achievement and business development and employability in the region. The population growth in the area will evidently only worsen the ratio of those without educational qualifications and/or employment, so the expanding population (albeit at a fairly steady rate of growth) needs to be supported by the rural renewal projects. The expansion of the university in the area will also drive up both levels of educational attainment and diversify employability, though such ideals need to be supported by the creation and development of businesses in the area, broadening existing employment in the educational and public sectors. The projects are also focused on integrating the leadership of communities and developing strengths in areas such as civic and governmental institutions, and growing the tourism and private sectors.

Key issues such as educational attainment, health and mortality rates are long-standing and underpinning issues in the need for rural renewal in the Eastern Cape. Focusing on each of these issues in more depth, the next section of the chapter moves on to examine the key roles of funders, actors and projects in the Eastern Cape.

Institutional context

In terms of the influence of underpinning institutional design, the key actors in driving and funding the projects are agencies delivering and funding the key priorities set at the national level. This demonstrates the important role of the key central agencies in working with the DLRDR in steering on behalf of national government and coordinating the constituent rural renewal projects. The targets, funding and setting of the governance partnership – including the themes of projects which may be funded – are decisions taken at the national level, setting the context of the roles of the actors engaged in delivery of the rural renewal projects.

Within the policy network, the power relations and respective roles are constructed by the national rather than state level, resulting in the construction of roles and the rules of engagement within the policy network by the actors in delivery. The roles of the other actors in the partnership are constructed by the role of national government as the key decision maker and funder, and the role of agencies close to government in coordinating the projects. The delivery of the projects by agencies on behalf of the centre has not been crowded out or constrained by the federal structure; rather, the broad range of partners and projects demonstrate the central steering and the construction of power relations.

Overview of key projects and partners

This section examines the projects' aims and objectives, and focuses on the partners in design and delivery of these rural renewal projects. The partners goals' are set out in the discussion below, drawing on the remit and strategic plan of the ECRDA. The role of the ECRDA is driven by working with both the DBSA and the range of partners in the region on specific themes and goals in the projects. As set out in the ECRDA's overview of their role, these themes are first set out below, and then discussed in terms of governance design. The ECRDA is engaged in a coordination and delivery role in these projects, focused on delivery on behalf of two government departments. These projects are focused on achieving targets over the short-term period:

> ECRDA is playing a social facilitation role on a number of forestry projects involving the departments of agriculture, forestry and fisheries (DAFF) as well as rural development and land reform (DRDLR).

There exists an opportunity to integrate existing DAFF plantations into new afforestation projects to increase economies of scale and offer the opportunity for immediate implementation during the delays of the forestry licensing process. The agency plans to plant 65,000 hectares of forestry plantations in the following five year period.

(Eastern Cape's Provincial Growth and Development Plan, 2008)

The governance design of these projects in Eastern Cape differs from other large-scale renewal projects in that the partnership and funding is not driven solely by the agencies or government departments. The funding is underpinned by a partnership with the Development Bank of Southern Africa (DBSA), designed to provide the impetus for the creation of jobs and business development:

ECRDA is equally proud that with the Eastern Cape Development Corporation (ECDC), the agency has entered into a R200 million Jobs Fund agreement with the Development Bank of Southern Africa (DBSA). This fund aims to empower local communities to participate and benefit from the local forestry developments as well as agro-processing thereby creating job opportunities and income streams. A total of R113 million of this amount has been allocated to forestry development.

(www.dedea.gov.za, 2013)

Within the Eastern Cape, there are several smaller flourishing projects. One such example is the local economic development agenda of the Nkonkobe municipality. Within Nkonkobe, the four areas that rural renewal centres on are: (i) agriculture, (ii) tourism, (iii) government and social sector, and (iv) whole and business sector. This approach in a small town setting mirrors the wider approach to rural renewal across projects in the Eastern Cape region. The focus on the four areas sets out to improve the economic context in Nkonkobe, and to build an identity and infrastructure as a vibrant university town with the university in the town of Alice, as part of the wider Alice regeneration strategy. This regeneration has developed from the rejuvenation programme in Alice, and is also informed by the Treasury and the ASPIRE small towns regeneration strategy – it emphasises three themes: building an engaged and sustainable community structure; investment; and becoming a university town, built around the University of Fort Hare (UFH). The Alice regeneration strategy, holistically, is wide ranging and ambitious, but, as with other rural renewal programmes in the area, is driven by partnership governance. As with several examples of both urban and rural renewal initiatives (and as detailed elsewhere in this book), the wide-ranging approach of the projects aims to improve and develop several areas (in the Eastern Cape instance, as we have seen, education, governance, business, and tourism). These areas, policy makers believe, necessitate a multi sectoral response by actors from different areas working together. In the Eastern Cape, this has expanded in some project areas beyond the public and private actors to include learning from international examples. The following sections examine the concept of learning across international examples between different local authorities: Oxfordshire in the UK, working with Nkonkobe, focuses on community leadership. The following sections examine this process, its focus and the concept of learning in rural renewal.

Oxfordshire and Ubuntu

The Eastern Cape partnership emphasises council partners in the region, but also illustrates the role of global learning and partnership. Oxfordshire County Council, together with funding from DfID, is engaged in projects exploring policy transfer and lesson drawing from the English city's experience. To be sure, Oxford is better equipped than most cities in terms of tourism expertise, and the county council and Oxford Brookes University are engaged with partners from the Eastern Cape in delivering a sustainable tourism strategy and also developing and strengthening community leadership. In terms of governance, this innovation brings partnerships on both sides together in Eastern Cape; focused on the principle of *Ubuntu* (meaning humanity or humaneness) the respective actors in this project are focused on tourism strategy, and are composed not only of public sector actors but also the private sector, with Adkins advising on architectural matters. The relations between actors in terms of governance here are far more structured than in many other rural renewal and development projects in the Eastern Cape. Funding from DfID from the UK national level, linked with a UK local authority, a UK University, and a private sector actor, and the local level Eastern Cape actors engaged with Oxfordshire forms a hierarchical 'partnership'. The key focus of knowledge exchange focuses on community leadership and embedding this ideal within the broader goal of sustainable communities, and also contributes to the notion of developing participation in the area, but in this process developing the civic and public life (participation in the area's politics and governance) in the area, both in terms of institutions and capacity. This partnership between Oxfordshire and Nkonkobe is an innovative example of governance exchange and aspects of policy transfer (though not the focus of this book, it should be noted that elements of partial policy exchange (Dolowitz and Marsh, 1998) exist in this example). The broader picture of governance partnership in achieving rural renewal in the Eastern Cape, as discussed at length later in this chapter, is a somewhat more complex picture.

Alice Regeneration Strategy

The context for Nkonkobe is reflected across the region in several areas which set the context for rural renewal. Within the Alice Regeneration Strategy, for example, are embedded several themes of educational attainment and employment. Moreover, across the projects in Nkonkobe, educational attainment levels are typically very low: 'The census data revealed that 13% of the Nkonkobe population has not attended school' (www. dedea.gov.za, 2013). Of the individuals in the region who do attend, only 14% leave with a qualification. This creates, as the Alice High Level Feasibility Assessment (2010) suggests, a two-tierism in the area between those who do not attend or attain, and those who are studying at the UFH. Similarly, the Feasibility Assessment argues that employment in the area is over dependent on the educational and wider public sectors for jobs. These routes, mainly the further education, higher education or public services/ governmental roles are at the heart of the Alice regeneration strategy in two ways. First, the need to increase community participation and infrastructure; and, second, the aim of business development among existing businesses and new start-ups. In terms of governance, Alice places an emphasis on community involvement, alongside the governmental (departments and agencies) engaged in delivering the Alice regeneration strategy. Building on the Business Case Report (2009) the Alice High Level Feasibility Assessment emphasises the following key themes:

- Provision of accommodation
- CBD upgrade and densification
- Sports and education
- Heritage development
- Functional integration
- Developing Local Agriculture

(Alice Regeneration Programme – High Level Feasibility Assessment Report, 2010)

What is the role of communities in the rural renewal projects?

These themes are driven by developing existing strength in Alice, such as sustainable communities, a university town, and economic and vibrant communities. Setting Alice and its rural renewal in the broader context of Nkonkobe and Eastern Cape, the area is 'a service centre and a university town nestled in the Tyume Valley, at the foothills of the Amatola Mountains, at the confluence of the Gaga and the Tyume Rivers' (Alice High Level Feasibility Assessment, 2010). Drawing on the key themes set out above, the rural renewal of Alice is focused on: (i) providing accommodation for students and professional people, (ii) upgrading the CBD, (iii) developing a sport and education zone, (iv) growing the ICT sector, and (v) heritage developments including a conference centre. These aspects of rural renewal focus on developing the key characteristics of Alice and also expanding areas for employment. The area has a strong focus and some success in terms of the community and social services sector, employing 44% of the workforce in Alice (Alice High Level Feasibility Assessment, 2010). Employment is also provided by the agricultural sector, which employs 13% of the workforce, and also private households (11% of the workforce). Much smaller employment is additionally provided by areas such as manufacturing and construction. There is also an underlying issue in Alice in that several households in the area are reliant on 'remittances, income from a single-wage earner and various small-scale activities' (Eastern Cape's Provincial Growth and Development Plan, 2008). There also exists an integration issue in Alice, as the area surrounding the university tends to be more educated and affluent, whereas the nearby villages tend to be poorer and show lower levels of educational attainment. The priorities set out above in the rural renewal projects in Alice show the aim of connecting the flourishing parts of the area to these less affluent areas, through the expansion of the CBD and tourism, as well as the heritage focus. The governance structure which underpins the rural renewal in Alice is driven by the Nkonkobe Municipal IDP (Alice High Level Feasibility Assessment, 2010) and, more broadly, in line with the Sector planning and the Eastern Cape's Provincial Growth and Development Plan (2008), the Amathole District Municipality Land Reform and Settlement Plan (2003), and the Nkonkobe Spatial Development Framework (2004). The rural renewal in Alice falls under the aegis of both Model 1 (urban) forms of development. Model 1 focuses on the north of Alice and Model 2 (rural) on the rural villages to the east of Alice. Regeneration in Alice, as part of the aim to grow the private and enterprise sector in the area, emphasises the role of expanding the retail sector, as well as the tourism, agricultural and property development sectors. Though there are examples of retail success in Alice, the expansion of this sector is needed to connect the poorer rural villages on the periphery of Alice with the more affluent (and urban) centre. By connecting the less affluent rural areas with the CBD, this enables the expansion of the CBD and greater transport linkage between the surrounding villages and the more urbanised areas of Alice. The delivery of this aspect of the programme would also drive expansion of the property market in Alice. The need to develop housing provision in Alice is driven by the low levels of housing in the area, and to provide infrastructure (together with improved transport links) for the increased CBD, college and university populations; and additionally provides a means of attracting young people to stay in the area, increasing the means of educational attainment and business life in Alice. The underpinning theme of achieving sustainable communities in a vibrant university town is contingent upon these related themes of housing, job creation and developing existing educational facilities and their role in life in Alice, achieving this infrastructure in the area would enable the creation of a more sustainable community. The example of Alice regeneration demonstrates the complexity of governance in the area. The regeneration strategy, as noted above, draws on earlier drafts and studies focused on planning and development strategy. These directly feed into the Alice regeneration strategy and its key themes.

The underpinning themes of these projects are to increase employment in the region, bolster tourism to the Eastern Cape, to increase public engagement and to further develop governance institutions. These aims are driven by a sustainability theme to improve development in an ecological manner, including agricultural business and development in the region. These themes are joined together in the aims of the projects, driven by the funding of government agencies and departments and a national bank. These actors, as will be discussed in more depth later on in this chapter, with reference to the interpretivist and policy networks governance frameworks. The chapter now moves on to examine the progress of the main projects in the Eastern Cape, examining the main actors engaged in funding, the costs of the projects, the time scale these aims and targets are working to, and the progress or outcome of these projects.

Who drives funding and delivery in the rural renewal projects? Rural renewal across the Eastern Cape: projects, funding and progress

The projects set out in Table 6.2 illustrate the key actors, funders and the outcomes and progress of the rural renewal programmes. The shift in who makes up this cast reveals changes in the patterns of governance as well as funders, and the role of the governance of the projects and the key actors in funding and delivery will be examined in detail in subsequent sections. Regarding the projects above, the most interesting role perhaps lies in that of the community. As noted earlier, the sustained engagement of local communities in regeneration projects was a central aim of the programme, in common with other rural and urban renewal programmes (such as Germany's Social City and the role of community as manager in project delivery (Shand, 2013)). The rural renewal programme, focused on building both enterprise and infrastructure located in historically poor areas of the region, with high mortality rates and similar levels of social exclusion, is driven by key partners such as large governance agencies in the projects, working with the local community and private sector actors in delivery, as well as acting as the funders.

Table 6.2 Outcomes and funding of projects in the Eastern Cape

Project/aim	Key actors, funding and outcomes
Forestry activity	The Eastern Cape aims to facilitate the establishment of 100,000 ha of new plantations and the rehabilitation of an existing 30,000 ha of plantations over the next 20 to 25 years. As plantations are established, opportunities for using raw material for various value-addition processes will be identified and implemented. ECRDA's role is to facilitate the establishment of community owned and managed forestry enterprises which are supported by suitable private sector operators.
Target plantations	There are currently five projects, 9,000 ha in extent, which are already operational. Over the past three years, 750 ha have been established within these projects, and a further 400 ha are planned for the 2013/2014 season. A total of R113 million has been secured from the DBSA Jobs Fund to finance eight projects over the next three years.
Target communities/ districts	Mkambati, Sinawo, Izinini, Gqukunka, Sixhotyeni are operational. Flagstaff, Lambasi and Maqhubini are at early stages of planning.
Potential for job creation	There are currently about 314 people employed. Over the next three years, 565 permanent jobs and 87 short-term jobs will be created.
ECRDA investment	ECRDA has committed R5.3 million to match the funding committed by the DBSA. The Jobs Fund has committed R83 million over the next three years on condition that R30 million of matched funding is in place. As such, an additional R24.7 million of matched funding is required over the next three years. At least R12 million is expected from ECRDA during 2014/2015 and 2015/2016. ECRDA intends to pull together public, social, financial and other resources that improve livelihoods while simultaneously developing sustainable rural economies and communities in the Eastern Cape. It seeks to leverage off strategic partnerships with the village being the centre of operation for a maximum and pronounced development impact

Source: www.ecrda.co.za, 2015.

The role of targets in network and partnership governance: New Public Management and New Public Governance

Responses to social and economic catastrophe, often ecological or environmental, have seen (in local, national and global examples) a focus on networks and partnerships, multi-agency or New Public Governance. However, implicit in each of these governance arrangements as responses to renewal programmes is the focus on targets. Why is this important? Conceptually, the enduring nature of new public management is evident in these processes. From a governance perspective there is a focus on targets and outcomes, certainly, but also on efficient management processes and delivery. Though seen as discredited by some scholars, the enduring nature of new public management is not only evident in the reluctance to abandon goals of efficiency and effectiveness, but rather that the idea of targets are the first solution to which we turn in the fight against vast underpinning social issues such as mortality, poor healthcare and low levels of educational attainment, as well as environmental degradation. Rural renewal is a joined-up response to these most problematic conflicts of ours and future eras. The reticence of New Public Management, and its stubbornness, lies in key aspects such as measurement, efficiency and targets.

First, the notion of measurement: locally, nationally and globally, governance responses to often large-scale social issues are driven by renewal programmes with the need to demonstrate both short-term and longer-term sustained improvement. This may be, some might suggest, for instrumental party political and electoral ends as well as the task of renewal, but this question is a matter for another debate. The importance of measurement, and the ease of communicating measurement, continues to be the value of NPM. This measurement, in the context of rural renewal as a policy response to underpinning and long standing social issues such as health, unemployment and low levels of educational attainment, enables communication across problems, sectors and borders: it enables the actors in the programme's design and delivery to (should they choose) encourage businesses to engage with communities and the development of civic institutions, adopt measures towards improved turnover, or healthcare, or housing. Why these specific examples in the context of rural renewal? They can be measured, and adopted, or enforced, across organisations which do not have borders, such as corporates.

The second enduring value of NPM is held in the related use of efficiency. Taking each of these aspects of NPM in turn, they possess value and suitability to rural renewal as a set of policy solutions and in the constituent underpinning social responses to this.

First, *measurement*: The role of targets in rural renewal tends to be focused on the longer term. Though there are some aspects of the Nkonkobe and Alice projects in the Eastern Cape which relate to targets around housing, for example, several of the underpinning themes of the regeneration focus on longer-term measures of sustainability. These relate to the focus on job creation, the identity of Alice and the notion of a more educated and engaged populace, as well as the overarching goal of achieving a sustainable community. Though each of these represents a target, these are less measurable goals as they are set in the longer term and in many cases, focused on increasing existing levels of attainment and employment rather than focusing on achieving x level by y year.

Second, *efficiency*: A cornerstone of NPM and the three Es (alongside economy and effectiveness) the notion of efficiency is crucial to measuring the success of the rural renewal projects: the number of educational qualifications; the residents in the area; the profits of local businesses in areas such as tourism and agriculture, and so on. To be sure, relying on these statistics blindly would represent a failure in terms of understanding the joined-up nature of rural renewal as a response to social problems. However, while the debate at a national and global level continues on issues such as mortality, economic development, environmental sustainability, and longer-term sustainable measures around the role of communities, the joined-up governance design continues to drive policy. Related to the discussion of measurement above, the role of efficiency is also hard to ascertain in the Eastern Cape rural renewal initiative. To be sure, no government wants to waste resources. We have seen significant investment in the area for rural renewal from government departments, a government agency overseeing the rural regeneration projects and from a national bank. This cross sectoral support for the regeneration of the Eastern Cape is also underpinned by linage with a range of existing businesses, civic organisations and community groups.

Third, *targets*: The focus at the heart of NPM is achieving targets, as a demonstrable means of progress and of comparison, across time, geographies and sectors. The role of targets is the key aspect of the enduring nature of new public management. Indeed, as suggested in this book, targets have remained the central aspect of both policy design and delivery. As illustrated throughout this book, the role of targets in achieving and measuring short-term and more sustained successful outcomes has been an enduring one – they are replicable and comparable, both across time and space. Furthermore, to achieve success in the aims of rural renewal in the Eastern Cape, and its responses to local regional and national issues, we need to look at the governance model. Nationally and globally, we have seen partnership and network governance in several policy areas in the last decade. This advent of the New Public Governance approach (Osborne, 2010) has seen a large focus on coordinated design and delivery, and has been argued by some to have displaced NPM. However, though NPM has somewhat drifted out of fashion in some debates, in practice we see both partnership and targets. In multi-agency settings, we see an emphasis on joined up response and delivery, but we do not see a reduction in focus on targets and efficiency, and through this, the endurance of NPM. As mentioned earlier in this chapter, debates in the academy about shifting from a focus on NPM to NPG do not reduce the focus on targets and measurability of outcomes. Though we see a preponderance of partnership or network approaches to governance, the role of targets often remains central to the aims of these groups of actors (and equally, each actor has their own set of targets and priorities which can cause issues in communication across the partnership or network). The Alice and Nkonkobe renewal projects in the Eastern Cape both display rural and urban elements to their goals, and, as such, the partnership governance response to these renewals is couched in both urban and rural renewal. However, the focus in these areas is mainly upon rural themes. The partnership focus is apparent in each of these themes: funded by large government agencies set up by government departments, working in collaboration in delivery with banks and smaller actors such as community groups. However, though the enduring nature of targets is apparent in this (and many other) governance partnership arrangements, the differing size, role and capacity of the constituent actors means their respective roles also have an effect on the way they interact in the partnership.

Drawing upon Figure 6.1, in the Eastern Cape this demonstrates how different actors interpret their roles in the partnership, how they interpret those of other actors and how these notions in turn then affect the way they carry out and view their own role. As discussed in Chapter 2, this interpretation draws upon ideas of role and interpretation, as well as Mead (1934) and Bevir (2008, 2011) in stating the importance of the construction of actor A's role by actor A in relation to how they see actor B's role in relation to their own. This construction tends to be driven by differences in power, resources, organisation, proximity to government, and (in some cases) individual role. However, such a philosophical approach only generates practical meaning when these constructions are driven by issues such as rank, organisation and resources. For example, where there are governmental actors in the network (or partnership) the roles are defined by size and budget as much as by history.

The following annotation in Figure 6.2 and subsequent discussion unpacks these themes, focused on the actors in the design and delivery of rural renewal projects in the Eastern Cape, and the relations between them and the learning from governance responses. In developing a more robust understanding of governance, and as noted in the methodological Chapter 3, this research seeks to develop a model which facilitates and enables more proactive rather than reactive action in mitigation of climate change. In achieving this aim, the governance model revisits the notion of networks, which are still in evidence from public services' responses to regeneration and development programmes through multi-agency working. The

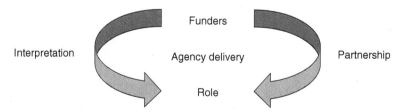

Figure 6.1 Roles and interpretations in governance networks and partnerships in the Eastern Cape.

model in this book builds on failures in network delivery in previous regeneration and sustainability policy programmes which were too bloated, large and uncoordinated (Shand, 2013) and also the concept of efficiency and management across public and private sectors to avoid communication breakdown or duplication of roles. The model seeks to unite the strengths of the response in the design and delivery of rural regeneration in the Eastern Cape – support for local business among the community, effective public engagement and institutional capacity – with a more proactive and connected linkage to bottom up community business development and participation and to contribute in comparative analysis to lesson drawing from other national examples and theory. The model will illustrate the findings in the Eastern Cape, focused on the projects in Alice and Nkonkobe, in relation to power relations and differences in roles between the actors and across the network or partnership arrangement as a whole, drawing on both more behavioural policy networks thinking and also discussions of how this contributes to power relations such as inequalities between these different actors in 'partnership' and in the governance and delivery of rural renewal, with the research providing an analysis of these relations between actors in the model and of understanding these processes, as in the preceding empirical case study chapters.

Modelling the findings

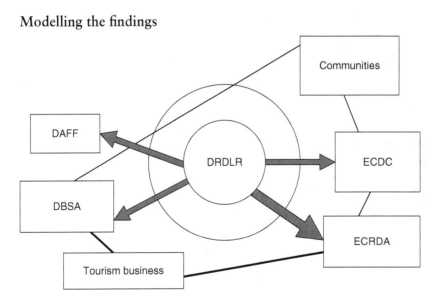

Figure 6.2 Network governance and partnership model in the Eastern Cape.

Who are the relevant stakeholders in the rural renewal projects?

The partnership governance model in Figure 6.2 has previously been applied to large-scale urban renewal projects across city regions in different countries (Shand, 2013), in the UK (Thames Gateway), Germany (Social City), and in the USA (Portland and Bridgeport). In this book, applying the same model as a proposition to similar scale projects in the Eastern Cape, the model sets out to examine and chart the relations between actors in the rural renewal initiative, in terms of power, resources and delivery (i.e. who does what), and draws upon interpretivist governance in examining this in the subsequent sections.

The network governance model in Figure 6.2 applied to the Eastern Cape demonstrates the main actors and their relations, driven by funding and delivery. The governance of rural renewal projects in the Eastern Cape is driven by delivery and funds from government departments and the financial sector. These actors – notably DAFF, BCDC, and DRDLR – work with DBSA from the banking sector and ECRDA in coordination and delivery, as well as a primary role from both of these actors (DBSA and ECRPA) in funding and targeting projects (as set out in Table 6.2). These relations between these major actors are demonstrated by the stronger connections in Figure 6.2, with the arrows denoting the direction of travel from funding in the projects. The smaller partners are illustrated in the Eastern Cape network governance model in Figure 6.2 by smaller, lighter connecting lines. These actors, such as local businesses, community groups and farmers, are connected to these larger governmental actors, and are engaged in projects funded typically by the DBSA and ECRPA, focused on community engagement, job creation and attracting and developing local rural businesses in the region. The partnership demonstrates clear asymmetries, though we need to unpack how hierarchies and power operate in and across this governance model.

First, let us look at the issue of *funding*. The source and direction of funding in the rural renewal projects overwhelmingly comes from two types of sources. These are government departments and agencies, and the banking sector. This national level direction illustrates the top down relations in terms of funding to projects and actors. The delivery of projects, however, is more heterarchical. The actors engaged in delivery show a more bottom-up approach to delivery of rural renewal – necessitated by local knowledge and existing work in, for example, areas such as tourism. Where the hierarchy meets these existing actors is the direction and coordination of targets and strategies in realising the rural renewal projects. Turning to the smaller actors in Figure 6.2, many of these are joined up through the projects (though some actors have relationships which are not dependent on funding).

Partners or networks: roles, power and who governs?

Applying policy networks thinking, there are some consistent elements of disaggregation (as in the DPM) throughout both design and delivery in the projects (as in, funding is driven by agencies); however, importantly in terms of these theoretical approaches, the power relations through funding and resource channels denote hierarchy and direction, and an asymmetry to relations (as in the APM). Drawing on Bevir's thinking, and on Figure 6.1, the relations between actors in the governance structure are influenced by power: the interpretations of actors and their respective roles are driven by the need to resource projects and to satisfy targets. Furthermore, the majority of funding is coming from government agencies, illustrating a clear asymmetry in power relations across the network or 'partnership'. These roles are reinforced by the size and scope of the actor – a department as part of government; or an agency created by government to deliver the rural renewal initiative, are evidently larger and more powerful than community groups or small businesses in the region. These differences in role are reflected through the financial muscle in the partnership. Though there is a degree of hollowing out and differentiation in the model driven by the presence of agencies and their coordinating and funding role, the role of government departments underpinning these actors demonstrates the notion of 'hands off, but at arm's length' (Taylor, 2000). Where we see the presence of actors such as DAFF, ECDC, DRDLR and ECRDA in the network, these are the largest actors and as these are governmental actors (departments and agencies), they are at the heart of the target setting, funding but also coordinating the projects. As such, these actions and remit reinforce the construction of these actors' roles as powerful and the smaller actors' roles in relation to these governmental actors as resource dependent, which drives the projects in terms of targets but also in terms of actors' behaviour, in reinforcing the mutual construction and interpretation of power relations and inequalities across the network.

That power relations and roles in the notion of partnerships are constructed and driven by the funding and resource awarding bodies

As the empirics of the projects set out in Table 6.2 illustrate, these actors were involved heavily (in common with aspects of the other rural renewal cases in this book but also similar urban renewal and development projects in Canada, the UK and the USA) but latterly there is evidently a shift towards private sector companies and communities – through the building and management of civic and public institutions – taking on more responsibility in delivery, and therefore in maintaining the longer-term outcomes and the sustainability of the programme.

In the Eastern Cape, there is an emphasis on providing infrastructure to facilitate behaviour change: there are (too) many regeneration and development programmes foreground models which emphasise development of housing and business. Such emphasis misses the point in terms of the holistic nature of regeneration – existing communities need to be engaged, rather than simply displaced. The projects in Alice and Nkonkobe in the Eastern Cape are excellent examples of holistic strategies. Though the aims of the projects are ambitious, they are also clear: importantly, there is a clear, consistent linkage between the private and public spheres. The development of businesses and the tourism industry is not only matched by infrastructure to accommodate and support this (the conference centre, transport links, housing) there is also a consistent linkage to increasing facilities and participation for existing communities in these areas, through expansion of educational facilities (both further and higher education) and governance, and through building on strengths in civic and public life. Indeed, this linkage is embedded in the aims and through each of the projects to achieve sustainable communities in the Eastern Cape. Sustainable communities are a goal many (urban and rural) renewal initiatives reach for, but the need to embed growth with participation from the current residents is one which is too seldom achieved. The sustainable communities focus is essential, and at the heart of the rural renewal in these areas. In Alice, for example, the University community is more transient than a village community on the edge of the area. Linking these together unites education, infrastructure, transport, business and employability, to be sure, but it also drives the most pressing issue for any policy maker or governance agency in regeneration – how will it grow in the future?

Conclusions in the Eastern Cape

This chapter has set out the findings in the Eastern Cape, which show that the hypothesis was correct. The Eastern Cape, and the projects focused upon in this chapter within Nkonkobe and Alice, driven by educational, transportation, and public and private infrastructure development, requires a more complex map of actors than simply government departments, governance agencies and businesses. This is due to a greater number of agency actors, driven by the ECDC and the ECRDA.

The Eastern Cape case study saw a joined-up response from public and private services and corporates in responding to the rural renewal programmes. However, two lessons can be learned from these examples that have resonance both for the Eastern Cape and in transferring the learning and governance from this project to other cases. First, the response in the Eastern Cape, both in Alice and Nkonkobe, from both public services and the private sector locally, saw common themes and a strong base of community support. Second, the academic literature in public policy and politics has (after much debate) shifted away from the notion of governance networks (inter alia, Taylor, 2000) and related New Public Governance (Osborne, 2010) ideas as workable solutions. However, ideas that form part of these debates are still operating in practice, such as joined-up or multi agency working across rural renewal and development programmes. In terms of systems change, and as noted above, there is a gap between public and private progress and development in the projects which is a longer-term theme to be addressed, and additionally in bringing together a co-ordinating governance mechanism for public and private services, with the communities then engaged in managing and delivering public policy. The rural renewal projects need both the public and private areas of focus to succeed, and to create linkage between these areas in terms of attracting people to the area and increasing employability in the Eastern Cape. The governance of the rural renewal initiative shows the dependence on large governance agencies acting on behalf of the central government departments to fund, coordinate and deliver projects and, longer term, the success in outcomes in rural renewal will be focused on the ability of public and private developments and an expanding population to maintain these services and finances.

The major actors in the governance partnership in the Eastern Cape, such as the ECRDA and ECDC, have a prominent role in the funding and coordination of the rural renewal projects, demonstrating the importance of agencies in collaboration and delivery. The major relations within the partnership take place between the governance agencies, acting on behalf of the centre, working with community groups and the private sector organisations already demonstrating growth and excellence in the Eastern Cape. The development of these businesses and public services – particularly those of education, housing and transport – are crucial to achieving short-term success in the project aims but also, even more vitally, in embedding this improved infrastructure across the Eastern Cape in the longer term to achieve the sustainability which is emphasised in the rural renewal agenda, in terms of areas such as transport, economic development and financial sector, and the ecological and environmental aspects of embedded sustainability across the Eastern Cape.

This represents one of the key themes of the chapter, both in terms of the academic literature and the conceptual approaches of governance, each linked to practice. The relationship between these actors is examined drawing upon the interpretivist approach, arguing that some community actors have assumed – accidentally – the role of governance. These organisations have undertaken regeneration projects, been responsible for community engagement within them, and have set targets and funding levels linked to regeneration initiatives such as improving neighbourhood safety, social and educational activities, or other community-based aspects of the programmes.

Key themes in the Eastern Cape

- Large amount of coordination and delivery from agencies
- Focus on community engagement in rural renewal projects and on the role of community in longer sustainable success, notably in civic institutions and business
- Focus on growing numbers of younger people staying and moving to the region

7 USA
North Dakota

This chapter examines the fourth case study area. This US case study, North Dakota, is driven by key partnerships involving the agricultural, business, governmental and educational sectors. Technological innovation and community involvement in the region in driving rural development have an important influence in the region and existing businesses, working towards tourism and connectedness of the area. Historically, this has taken place in areas such as telecommunications, entrepreneurship more broadly and in agriculture. However, the enduring themes of these rural renewal and development initiatives in North Dakota have been underpinned by the notion of partnership or collaborative approaches to the governance of these projects; and have also focused on the importance of the community as a key actor in these partnerships. These themes hold true in the rural renewal (and its governance) projects across North Dakota examined in this chapter. The chapter begins by setting out the social context for rural renewal in North Dakota, examining the key demographic trends and areas of need, such as the age of the population, educational attainment, and health and housing needs, as well as issues such as transport and employability. The chapter then moves on to examine the recent history of rural renewal and development in North Dakota, before focusing on some of the key current projects in rural renewal. Finally, the chapter examines the key actors in governance, modelling these in terms of the governance partnership, and focusing on the roles of key actors, funding, and relations between the actors, such as governance agencies, businesses and community groups. These will be examined in terms of power, functionality, funding, interaction and decision-making. Let us first turn to the underpinning social context of North Dakota, and how such key trends and needs act as drivers for rural renewal in the area.

Social demographics for rural renewal in North Dakota

Looking at the demographic statistics in Table 7.1, the key underpinning themes of the rural renewal projects across North Dakota become evident. The need to develop infrastructure, healthcare and business are

Table 7.1 Socio-economic data for North Dakota

Population	
Population, 2014 estimate	739,482
Population, 2010 (April 1) estimates base	672,591
Population change – 1 April 2010 to 1 July 2014 (%)	9.9
Population, 2010	672,591
Persons under 5 years, 2014 (%)	6.9
Persons under 18 years, 2014 (%)	22.8
Persons 65 years and over, 2014 (%)	14.2
Female persons, 2014 (%)	48.7
Housing	
Median value of owner-occupied housing units, 2009–2013	$132,400
Households, 2009–2013	287,270
Persons per household, 2009–2013	2.31
Per capita money income in past 12 months ($2013), 2009–2013	$29,732
Median household income, 2009–2013	$53,741
Persons below poverty level, 2009–2013 (%)	11.9
No. of residents with no formal academic qualifications	
High school graduate or higher, age 25+, 2009–2013 (%)	90.9
Bachelor's degree or higher, age 25+, 2009–2013 (%)	27.2
Number of firms	
Total number of firms, 2007	61,546
Black-owned firms, 2007 (%)	0.3
American Indian- and Alaska Native-owned firms, 2007 (%)	1.6
Asian-owned firms, 2007 (%)	0.7
Native Hawaiian and Other Pacific Islander-owned firms, 2007 (%)	0.0
Hispanic-owned firms, 2007 (%)	0.5
Women-owned firms, 2007 (%)	24.8
Non-farming enterprise	
Private non-farm establishments, 2013	24,088
Private non-farm employment, 2013	342,747
Private non-farm employment change, 2012–2013 (%)	3.5
Non-employer establishments, 2013	51,879

Source: www.commerce.nd.gov, 2015.

key to building the private sector across North Dakota in addition to developing existing expertise around farming and agriculture. The number of residents with educational qualifications at degree level is one quarter of the population, leading to the need to retain and attract talented and younger people in the North Dakota area, and to develop facilities to enable this to happen in the longer term, is a key driver for rural renewal across both public and private areas of investment across rural renewal in North Dakota. The need to establish greater technological capacity through connectivity is an obvious underpinning need to achieve in the short term in order to achieve a better structure for businesses to develop across North Dakota. Similarly, the need to expand upon public sector service areas such as housing, healthcare and transport is a key aim of the rural renewal programme. The development and expansion of these areas of public provision is not only a central aim in developing infrastructure for the existing community, but also vital in attracting people to stay in the area or to move to North Dakota, raising levels of education, business development – including supporting existing expertise in areas such as agriculture – and civic infrastructure.

What is the sustainability of the rural renewal projects?

Historically, the focus of rural development in the North Dakota area has focused upon: the role of businesses and in encouraging entrepreneurship; in building technology and capacity; and in the development of civic and public institutions. This focus has been one born out of a need for connectivity and of attracting residents to the region, and in building employability. These ideas have, to an extent, involved delivery by joined-up or collaborative approaches, which have embedded the community in delivery, or linked the community in the area to business development strategies. These projects have echoes in many aspects of the rural renewal programme and its governance design and delivery. First, the notion of collaboration or partnership is embedded through the large number of actors involved in rural renewal and development in North Dakota (discussed in more depth in the latter sections of this chapter). Second, a key aspect of this partnership approach is the connectedness of the local community to the rural renewal projects. And, third, the key themes that arise from the rural renewal and development projects in the North Dakota area: in the projects there remains a link with past projects that have focused on issues of community engagement, farming and agriculture, and technological development and connectivity. The key themes that have resonance with the on-going rural development and renewal work in North Dakota can be characterised as (i) the history of collaborative and partnership governance approach in North Dakota, (ii) the role of entrepreneurship, technology and connectivity in past projects, and (iii) the role of communities in the partnership approach. Let us now look at each of these influences in turn.

History of collaborative and partnership governance approach in North Dakota: This focus has been used to an extent in rural development projects in terms of collaboration or cooperatives, which have been used to drive rural development at a time when there was population and employability decline in rural areas of North Dakota. As Bhuyan and Olson (1998) argue, the rural geography of some of these communities necessitated organisation and collaboration:

> Declining population and business, compounded by declining state and federal funding, put financial stress on these communities to provide

and maintain services such as grocery stores or supermarkets, local credit/banking facilities, rural emergency health services, garbage disposal, and other retail and service related outlets.

(Bhuyan and Olson, 1998: iii)

The notion of cooperatives in North Dakota was driven by the need to support areas of commerce and industry, as well as civic and public life that were in need of infrastructure for local communities. These areas of need tended to be removed from industries in North Dakota like agriculture, and focused on the development of service sector and private sector capacity building to address local community need and to deliver growth. This cooperative approach, Bhuyan and Olson (1996, 1998) go on to argue, addressed these needs and was also the subject of an NDSA funded pilot in 1997. The role of communities in the pilot study integrated the notion of communities in collaboration in governance of rural development and renewal. The integration of communities with businesses and the service sector in this pilot, suggest Bhuyan and Olson (1998), was a learning experience for the communities engaged with the project, but one that they found a learning process. The role of the community was a vital one as part of the cooperative, in terms of its legitimacy and its ownership of the renewal and development – such as business expansion or agricultural regeneration – and moreover, in embedding the role of the community in the design and delivery of the rural renewal projects in North Dakota. These cooperatives, during the 1990s, created a participatory function for communities in terms of the development of their area, particularly in regard to the expansion of services, commerce and businesses. However, North Dakota has also seen cooperatives employed in relation to the agricultural sector, notably the 'new generation cooperatives' (Harris et al., 1996) that worked on several aspects of farming and production in the area:

New Generation Cooperative (NGC) is the term that has been applied to the dozens of value-added processing, selected membership cooperatives that have formed in the North Dakota and Minnesota area ... the new cooperatives have sprung up in virtually every sector of agricultural production in the region.

(Egerstrom, 1994; Harris et al., 1996)

The role of entrepreneurship, technology and connectivity in past projects: Across previous rural renewal and development projects in North Dakota, the focus on business development and enlargement, technological innovation and upgrades, and connecting communities (and their businesses) lead to improved technological infrastructure and capacity. These themes are reflected in the projects in the rural renewal programme in North Dakota, demonstrating the historical need to improve these aspects of delivery in the area. In addition, rural renewal in North Dakota is driven by the development of areas of public service and public life; the improvement of food and water, transport and particularly healthcare is a key focus of renewal.

The role of communities in the partnership approach: The focus on healthcare development is, once again, one that has been apparent in previous rural development initiatives. The federal and national levels have driven this. The need to develop health services, underpinned by the social context and statistics discussed at the beginning of this chapter is also an issue partly of connectivity. Rural areas like North Dakota in the US have historically experienced broader socio-economic factors that contribute to poorer levels of health among the local population such as lower levels of employment and more restricted access to services.

Indeed, historically, areas like healthcare have been seen as issues of isolation rather than health. As Cordes (1989) notes, this was driven by a notion that 'in earlier periods, the emphasis was on isolation – physical, social, economic, and cultural' (Cordes, 1989: 780). The effect of these socio-economic factors is evidently still the focus of rural renewal in North Dakota, particularly the need to increase employability and business development and digital literacy and connectivity. Cordes goes on to identify six characteristics of rural economies and how these relate to healthcare and health service delivery. In this vein, the underpinning characteristics which are integrated into the need for rural renewal and the resultant projects are: (i) rural economic structure, (ii) diversity of this rural economic structure, (iii) a specialised economic activity in the rural area or community, (iv) the interdependence and integration of the rural economy with the national and global economies, (v) the vulnerability and uncertainty of the rural economies due to the interdependence on these external factors, and (vi) each of these factors are new developments in rural economies (Cordes, 1989: 780).

The rural renewal programme in North Dakota continues to emphasise healthcare and the development of infrastructure to combat related issues such as those set out above – low levels of employability or economic activity, high levels of poverty, and low levels of connectivity to resources and digitally. The focus on healthcare and services in the rural renewal projects has seen spending by the USDA and fundraising by the local community. An example of this is the construction of the new hospital in Bowman, following a $15 million loan from the USDA via its communities facilities program, and $3.7 million worth of community fundraising, towards the total cost of $25 million. The aim is to complete this construction by the end of 2016, with employment in the facility another key target:

> the project will be a two-storey structure allowing for expansion to go upward with future growth. Southwest Healthcare Services is the

largest employer in Bowman with a staff of more than 180 people. They have plans to hire additional employees after construction is finished.

(USDA Rural Development Healthcare, 2014)

The investment is aimed at solving health issues of access and connectivity, driven by population need and also population increase:

> Access to rural health services is critical to growing a sustainable community. As North Dakota's population continues to rise, pressure is put on medical and emergency services. To help, USDA Rural Development has enhanced projects such as: state-of-the-art healthcare facilities so people have access to the highest level of care; long term care facilities so seniors could live closer to their families; and wellness and emergency service centers so rural areas remained attractive places to live and work.
>
> (USDA Rural Development Healthcare, 2014)

Who are the relevant stakeholders in the rural renewal projects? The role of USDA Rural Development

The USDA Rural Development (USDA RD) is the central focal point in delivery and funding of rural renewal projects across North Dakota. It encompasses funding and grants for projects in areas such as healthcare, housing and communications. More broadly, the USDA RD has, in terms of rural renewal, several areas of interest and includes two programmes that deliver funding and loans to communities and businesses engaged in rural renewal projects across North Dakota. In focusing first on the community side of these funding initiatives, the

> Sustainable Community Development advances the creation of liveable and vibrant communities through comprehensive approaches that coordinate economic, environmental, and community development. Essential community infrastructure is key in ensuring that rural areas enjoy the same basic quality of life and services enjoyed by those in urban areas. Community Facilities Programs offer direct loans, loan guarantees and grants to develop or improve essential public services and facilities in communities across rural America. These amenities help increase the competitiveness of rural communities in attracting and retaining businesses that provide employment and services for their residents. Public bodies, non-profit organizations and federally recognized American Indian Tribes can use the funds to construct, expand or improve facilities that provide health care, education, public safety, and public services. Projects include fire and rescue stations, village and town halls, health care clinics, hospitals, adult and child

care centers, assisted living facilities, rehabilitation centers, public buildings, schools, libraries, and many other community based initiatives. Financing may also cover the costs for land acquisition, professional fees, and purchase of equipment. These facilities not only improve the basic quality of life, and assist in the development and sustainability of rural America.

(USDA RD, 2015)

The USDA RD also focuses on the role of building infrastructure in existing communities and also develops the role of the community actor in participation and engagement in governance process of the rural renewal projects. The community actor is driven by the notion of community-based partnerships, again emphasising the notion of partnership working in governance and delivery and focusing on the collaboration between sectors such as the public, private and voluntary and achieving community participation with the key aims of rural renewal projects reflected in this broad scope of the different professions and interests which make up the community. The focus on the community as partners in the governance process is also intend to drive participation in projects around building public infrastructure such as healthcare, creating a more sustainable community structure in the longer term.

> The Strategic Vision for Change identifies what a community will become in the future and a statement of the values in which the community used to create its "vision". The Community-Based Partnerships principle encourages all stakeholders in a community to participate in the revitalization of distressed neighborhoods, including residents, businesses, local political leaders, community development corporations, and other community groups.
>
> (USDA RD, 2015)

- Health care facilities such as hospitals, medical clinics, dental clinics, nursing homes or assisted living facilities
- Public facilities such as town halls, courthouses, airport hangars or street improvements
- Community support services such as child care centers, community centers, fairgrounds or transitional housing
- Public safety services such as fire departments, police stations, prisons, police vehicles, fire trucks, public works vehicles or equipment
- Educational services such as museums, libraries or private schools
- Utility services such as telemedicine or distance learning equipment
- Local food systems such as community gardens, food pantries, community kitchens, food banks, food hubs or greenhouses

(USDA RD, 2015)

The role of Rural Community Development Initiative Grants in rural renewal projects: The role of community grants is central to the design and delivery of a wide range of projects across North Dakota. In terms of the scope and eligibility of these awards, there is a focus on 'Public bodies, Non-profit organizations, and Federally Recognized Tribes' (USDA RD, 2015) Funded project areas can include

> Rural areas including cities, villages, townships, towns and Federally Recognized Tribal Lands outside the boundaries of a city of 50,000 or more and its immediately adjacent urbanized area.... To improve housing, community facilities, and community and economic development projects in rural areas.
>
> (USDA RD, 2015)

Funding for these grants ranges from $50,000 to $250,000, and these are awarded to successful rural renewal projects in competition. Rural Community Development Initiative grants can include themes such as:

Training sub-grantees to conduct:

1   Home-ownership education
2   Minority business entrepreneur education

Providing technical assistance to sub-grantees on:

1   Strategic plan development
2   Accessing alternative funding sources
3   Board training
4   Developing successful child care facilities
5   Creating training tools, such as videos, workbooks, and reference guides
6   Effective fundraising techniques

(USDA RD, 2015)

Institutional context

In terms of institutional design, the key actors in driving and funding the projects are agencies driven by funds and priorities set at the national (rather than at North Dakota state) level. This demonstrates the important role of the key central agencies in steering the constituent rural renewal projects to the coordinated national agenda. The priorities, funding and setting of the governance partnership – including the themes of projects which may be funded – are decisions taken at the national level, setting the context of the roles of the actors engaged in delivery of the rural renewal projects.

The governance power relations and respective roles are then ascribed by the national rather than state level, and the construction of roles and the rules of engagement within the policy network are created. The roles of the other actors in the partnership are constructed by the role of national government as the key decision maker and funder, through the USDA RD agency. The delivery of the projects by agencies on behalf of the centre has not been crowded out or constrained by the federal structure, with the role of the agency in North Dakota one of a similar role with many states in delivery of the national rural renewal programme.

Where there are specific bodies established to represent the community, these can also be set up by the national level: the role of the North Dakota Rural Development Council discussed below, is one such example, with this being a national initiative.

North Dakota Rural Development Council (ND RDC)

Across North Dakota, working with the other key actors in the governance partnership such as the USDA RD, is the North Dakota Rural Development Council. The role of the ND RDC is to engage in partnership with public and private sectors in the communities across the North Dakota state. The role of the ND RDC – as part of the National Rural Development Partnership Program – is to draw together the diverse sectors of communities and to aid them in engaging with the governance process, notably in enabling successful coordination and communication between diverse actors, to avoid the issues such as communication, role confusion and competition which can arise in multi-agency working or in New Public Governance arrangements (Osborne, 2010).

North Dakota Rural Development Council (ND RDC) is North Dakota's chapter of the National Rural Development Partnership Program. The Council is an active partnership uniting the state's private and non-profit sectors and state, federal, local and tribal governments in an effort to strengthen rural America.

Mission
To strengthen rural North Dakota's capacity for growth, the council works to connect private and non-profit sectors of local, state, federal, tribal and community-based organizations to resolve or eliminate overlapping services through communication and cooperation.
Our state council works to:

- Facilitate collaboration among federal, state, local, and tribal governments and the private and nonprofit sectors in the planning and implementation of programs and policies that have an impact on rural areas of the state.

- Monitor, report, and comment on policies and programs that address, or fail to address, the needs of the rural areas of the state.
- Facilitate the development of strategies to reduce or eliminate conflicting or duplicative administrative or regulatory requirements of federal, state, local, and tribal governments.

Goals
- Strengthen all North Dakotan's abilities to determine the future.
- Assist communities in determining and implementing local development objectives.
- Maximise limited resources through networks that help existing programs work effectively.
- Foster innovative solutions that eliminate barriers for rural development efforts.
- Create a communication network to unify public and private sector stakeholders.
- Develop relationships among rural citizens and all aspects of government.
- Ensure that benefits are widely shared among all rural citizens.
- Provide a forum through which pertinent issues, projects and activities are acted upon.

Keys to Success
- Collaboration & Coordination are the Keys to maximise limited resources.
- No one agency is in control of the council's direction.
- Regular succinct meetings keep members up to date on available, resources, needs and activities.

Source: http://trainingnd.com/rural-development/nd-rural-development-council

The role of the USDA RD in funding awards and grants reflects its main areas of function and delivery in the rural renewal across North Dakota. In common with the funding set out for communities, there is a similar fund available focused on business development, reflecting the key themes of the rural renewal initiative across North Dakota discussed earlier in this chapter, and the key drivers set out in the demographic and social context factors set out in the initial sections of this chapter. The Rural Business Development Grant, just as the community focused funding, is aimed at both developing existing enterprise in the North Dakota area and also at supporting smaller businesses. These grants reflect the role of the USDA RD as the central actor in funding and delivery of projects, working in partnership with public, private and community actors. The focus on public, community and private enterprise is reflected in the funding streams, and display important effects in coordination and delivery in terms of the power relations between actors and their roles in delivery:

Rural Business Development Grants (RBDG) (support) RBDG is a competitive grant designed to support targeted technical assistance, training and other activities leading to the development or expansion of small and emerging private businesses in rural areas that have fewer than 50 employees and less than $1 million in gross revenues. Programmatic activities are separated into enterprise or opportunity type grant activities.

(USDA RD, 2015)

Projects, progress and outcomes: key actors and funding in rural renewal in North Dakota

The key projects focused on by the USDA RD seek to develop themes such as broadband connectivity; Tribal Nations; health infrastructure in the community; environmental sustainability; and economic and business development. In addition to the key projects above, the USDA RD is also active in funding and overseeing rural renewal and development missions around areas such as the Single Family Housing Direct Home Loans and the Rural Business Development Grants, which are discussed in more detail in subsequent sections of this chapter. To be sure, this range of projects emphasises the holistic approach to rural renewal and development across North Dakota. The role of the USDA is also key in funding the majority of these projects. To achieve short-term success in outcomes, in common with many renewal and development large-scale initiatives, the projects and the holistic approach to renewal are focused on creating more sustainable infrastructure for future generations. For example, a key aspect of rural renewal is the need to create jobs through investment that will generate money in the area, attract new residents and encourage existing communities to stay. This investment is driven, as noted above, largely by investment into health, families, and business and broader public-private issues such as broadband connectivity. One such example of creating employability in North Dakota is the creation of a new manufacturing plant focused on agriculture. Funded by USDA RD, this plant enables local production and export of agricultural machinery to take place. Driven by a $5m loan, the plant opened in 2013 and has subsequently:

> The new 11,000 square foot plant was up and running in Mapleton, North Dakota, a small community of roughly 800 just west of Fargo. Production began with 40 new employees hired from around the region … the company anticipates growing business and adding employees in the Mapleton plant to 120 employees in the next three to five years.
>
> (USDA RD, 2015)

This example demonstrates key themes of the rural renewal programme in North Dakota more generally. First, the role of the USDA as funder; the

Table 7.2 Rural Business Development Grants (RBDG)

Who may apply for this program?
Rural public entities including, but not limited to:
- Towns
- Communities
- State agencies
- Authorities
- Nonprofit Corporations
- Institutions of Higher Education
- Federally-recognised Tribes
- Rural Cooperatives

What is an eligible area?
RBDG funds must be directed for projects benefitting rural areas or towns outside the urbanised periphery of any city with a population of 50,000 or more. Check eligible areas.

How much funding is available?
There is no maximum grant amount for enterprise type grants; however, smaller requests are given higher priority. Generally, grants range from $10,000 up to $500,000. There is no cost sharing requirement. Opportunity type grant funding is limited to a maximum award of $50,000 for unreserved funds. Total opportunity type grant funding is limited statutorily to up to 10% of the total RBDG annual funding.

How may funds be used?
Enterprise type grant funds must be used on projects to benefit small and emerging businesses in rural areas as specified in the grant application. Uses may include:
- Training and technical assistance, such as project planning, business counseling/training, market research, feasibility studies, professional/technical reports, or product/service improvements
- Acquisition or development of land, easements, or rights of way; construction, conversion, renovation, of buildings, plants, machinery, equipment, access streets and roads, parking areas, utilities
- Pollution control and abatement
- Capitalisation of revolving loan funds including funds that will make loans for start-ups and working capital
- Distance adult learning for job training and advancement
- Rural transportation improvement
- Community economic development
- Technology-based economic development
- Feasibility studies and business plans
- Leadership and entrepreneur training
- Rural business incubators
- Long-term business strategic planning

Opportunity type grant funding must be used for projects in rural areas and they can be used for:
- Community economic development
- Technology-based economic development
- Feasibility studies and business plans
- Leadership and entrepreneur training
- Rural business incubators
- Long-term business strategic planning

How are applications evaluated for competitive funding?
RBDG applications compete at the state office level, which are dependent on appropriations.

All applications are evaluated based on:
- Evidence showing job creation to occur with local businesses;
- Percent of nonfederal funding committed to the project;
- Economic need in the area to be served;
- Consistency with local economic development priorities;
- Experience of the grantee with similar efforts; and

Other factors described in the current Notice of Solicitation of Applications (NOSA), if one is published.

Funding is provided through a competitive process.
Direct Loan:
- Loan repayment terms may not be longer than the useful life of the facility, state statutes, the applicants authority, or a maximum of 40 years, whichever is less
- Interest rates are set by Rural Development, contact us for details and current rates
- Once the loan is approved, the interest rate is fixed for the entire term of the loan, and is determined by the median household income of the service area and population of the community
- There are no pre-payment penalties
- Contact us for details and current interest rates applicable for your project

Grant approval:
Applicant must be eligible for grant assistance, which is provided on a graduated scale with smaller communities with the lowest median household income being eligible for projects with a higher proportion of grant funds. Grant assistance is limited to the following percentages of eligible project costs:

1 Maximum of 75% when the proposed project is:
- Located in a rural community having a population of 5,000 or fewer; and
- The median household income of the proposed service area is below the higher of the poverty line or 60 percent of the State nonmetropolitan median household income.

2 Maximum of 55% when the proposed project is:
- Located in a rural community having a population of 12,000 or fewer; and
- The median household income of the proposed service area is below the higher of the poverty line or 70 percent of the State nonmetropolitan median household income.

3 Maximum of 35% when the proposed project is:
- Located in a rural community having a population of 20,000 or fewer; and
- The median household income of the proposed service area is below the higher of the poverty line or 80 percent of the State nonmetropolitan median household income.

4 Maximum of 15% when the proposed project is:
- Located in a rural community having a population of 20,000 or fewer; and
- The median household income of the proposed service area is below the higher of the poverty line or 90 percent of the State nonmetropolitan median household income. The proposed project must meet both percentage criteria. Grants are further limited:
- Grant funds must be available

Source: USDA RD, 2015.

linkage between the community and development of enterprise and business in the area; and the linkage to agriculture as a key area of success and which to grow in the longer term alongside the other key themes of the projects discussed earlier in the chapter, such as healthcare, infrastructure and the need to connect the North Dakota area through improved ICT access, focused on the development of faster Broadband and wider access and coverage of this project.

Overview of key projects and partners

The key actors in design and delivery in rural renewal and development projects in North Dakota are led by the USDA and within this agency, USDA Rural Development (USDA RD). The grants, loans and coordination of rural renewal projects are driven by the USDA RD with these funds being directed towards families, businesses and communities. The focus of USDA RD in North Dakota is divided into three agencies reflecting three strategic core areas of delivery. These are the Rural Housing Service, the Rural Business Service, and the Rural Utilities Service. Across these three agencies, there are forty programmes to deliver rural renewal in North Dakota. Annually, the USDA RD invests around $500 million in the area, reflecting a $3 billion loan portfolio in North Dakota. The USDA RD has six offices across the state, encompassing forty-two employees. The key projects focused on by the USDA RD seek to develop themes such as broadband connectivity; Tribal Nations; health infrastructure in the community; environmental sustainability; and economic and business development. Let us now look at North Dakota's rural renewal projects and aims in more detail.

The following sections now go on to model the roles and relations between the actors, in design, management and delivery of the rural renewal projects across North Dakota. The governance partnership model set out below examines the key actors as funders, partners and actors in terms of roles, power relations and delivery in the governance of rural renewal in North Dakota.

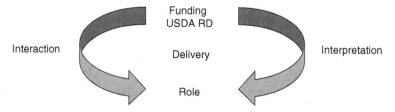

Figure 7.1 Roles and interpretations in governance networks and partnerships in North Dakota.

Table 7.3 Rural renewal projects and progress in North Dakota

Broadband connectivity: The need to invest in broadband infrastructure and increase digital connectivity in North Dakota is a key mission of rural renewal, and as discussed in the sections above, underpins a number of broader aims of the rural renewal programme, such as healthcare, business investment, and creating and nurturing sustainable communities in North Dakota. The need for investment in broadband to provide infrastructure for a growing population and also to attract greater numbers of people and talent to the area, and to foster business development.

Tribal Nations: During the period 2009–2013, the USDA invested more than $235 million in tribal nations in North Dakota, focusing on developing key elements such as: business and cooperative programs ($707,513); communities ($7.3 million); water and waste water ($17.4 million); electricals ($88.2 million); and telecommunications investment ($122 million).

Health in communities: Again, the USDA in North Dakota has been focused on areas such as clinics and hospitals ($125.65 million); longer term care investment ($44.82 million); investment in emergency vehicles and related facilities ($2.93 million); wellness ($4.05 million) and in investment in telemedicine ($574,400).

Water: Again, this initiative was underpinned by USDA investment. Funding since 2009 for water projects in North Dakota has totalled more than $97 million across 62 projects, in addition to other USDA funding. This funding has seen $58.6 million made in loans in addition to $38.7 million in grants. This funding has been directed at 26 cities and five water districts, as well as four Native American tribes. Broadly, the water projects funding from the USDA has reached 42,948 households and businesses.

Source: USDA RD, 2015.

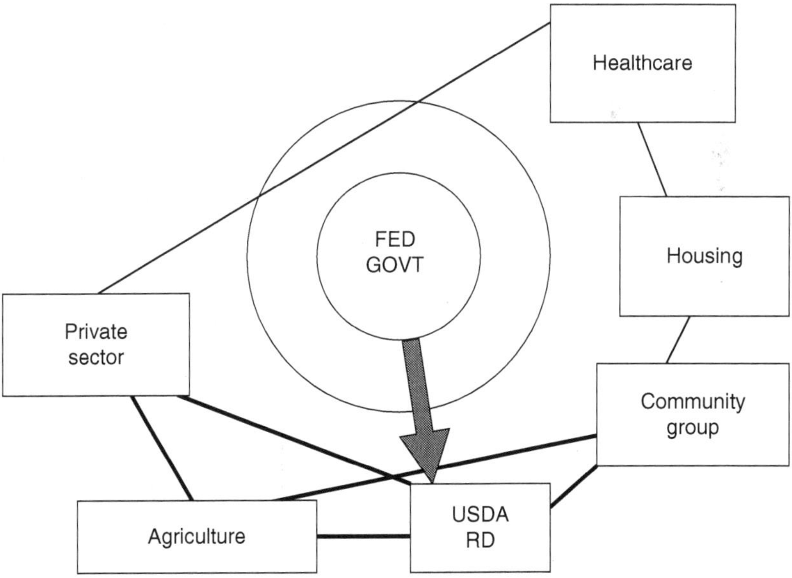

Figure 7.2 Network governance and partnership model in North Dakota.

Partners or networks: roles, power and who governs? Governance, partnerships and networks in rural renewal in North Dakota

Drawing upon the APM, the roles of actors in governance of rural renewal projects can be examined as set out in Figure 7.2 above. The asymmetry in governance relations – that is, the control and direction of projects priority and the related allocation of resources – is modelled by the direction and strength of connections. This asymmetry is illustrated in Figure 7.2 as these actors, with significant resources and autonomy in delivery of projects, are dependent on the will and resources of the central actors, such as the USDA RD. These relations between actors in decision making and resources for the rural renewal projects have implications for the respective roles of these actors and the resultant power relations across the governance partnership.

That power relations and roles in the notion of partnerships are constructed and driven by the funding and resource awarding bodies

The asymmetric relations between actors are illustrated by the directional flows of arrows to the major actors from the centre. The flows – of resources – are one-directional to emphasise the resource led steering of the USDA RD, though it could be argued that the expertise these agencies provide is a resource flowing back towards the centre. This is power of government and function in terms of delivery, however, as the government retains the power to remove this function and fill it in back to the centre. The major actors connected to the centre by bold arrows also show the flows of funding coming from the government to these large agencies. This illustrates the control of resources and priority exercised by the centre in the policy network, with these asymmetries in practice, as the resource flows of finance and decision making are illustrated as relations between the actors.

The model in Figure 7.2 illustrates the formal relations and roles of actors in governance. While we can still be sure that the debate is one of governance rather than government, given the centre's desire to dissolve bodies and create new ones, there is a question of how far governance takes place in a partnership sense. Though there is not sufficient space here to précis the entire literature on policy networks, key elements of which are discussed in Chapter 2, these debates can be considered subject to change. First, the notion of exchange of resources between actors may be changing, and the assumption of cooperation between actors may also be shifting towards a model whereby actors work in tandem with a private sector provider (and perhaps a government department). Though actors have always been subject to asymmetries and top down ad hoc creationism of bodies, the *number* of actors engaged in delivery has evidently shifted towards fewer actors and a far greater role for business. In terms of the idea of a policy network as a model, narrative (or even a realistic description!) of governance, the findings in North Dakota suggest that actors do cooperate, and that in relations in this partnership, there remains asymmetrical relations, rather than distinct hollowing out. To the extent where hollowing out has occurred, there have been major governance agencies engaged in funding and delivery in renewal, such as the USDA RD. This pattern, typified by the involvement of national-level agencies in funding (and in governance) illustrate a greater emphasis on the role of central agencies in delivery, and as noted earlier, the partnership model in governance is driven by the USDA RD in working with the community. As Marsh and Smith go on to note:

> Change is usually explained in terms exogenous to the network; as the external environmental changes it may affect the resources and interests of actors within a network. However, the extent and speed of change is clearly influenced by the network's capacity to mediate, and often minimize, the effect of such change. Networks are often faced by very strong external uncertainties and that does affect network structure, network interactions and policy outcomes.
>
> (2000: 8)

As Marsh then suggests:

> The asymmetric power model also sees the relationship between institutions and ideas as dialectical ... it argues that there is a dominant political tradition in the UK, based on a limited liberal notion of representation and a conservative notion of responsibility, which underpins the institutions and processes of British politics.
>
> (Marsh, 2011: 42)

The role of interpretation of roles in the governance partnership, accepting the inequalities and differences between them, has effects on communication and collaboration; these roles are also limited by motivations, histories and existing partnerships. These effects on actors emphasise the range of 'structures that constrain and facilitate agents' (Marsh, 2008: 737).

Sorensen (2002) Marsh and others draw upon the notion of metagovernance in governance networks of the power relations and roles of actors which are shaped of government refracted through favoured or created bodies. The notion of metagovernance in collaborative governance arrangements, such as networks or partnerships, suggests that with a greater number of actors there is a problem of interpretation of roles. Crucially, there is also the risk of partnerships or networks acting as barriers to public accountability or the interactivity of the network with communities. However, the central focus on the role of communities in rural renewal projects across North Dakota is an important mechanism of engagement and interactivity in the partnership. Though the actors do not occupy the same roles, and scholars may suggest that the partnership is founded on unequal roles (and is not therefore a pluralistic partnership), the role of partnership can also be seen through the lens of political story-telling. Though the role of communities is one which is foregrounded in the design and delivery of the governance partnership in the rural renewal, the political storytelling around this theme could be seen critically as one which does not reflect the roles and power relations in the composition of the governance partnership. However, as noted above, the community is represented through organisations such as the ND RDC and in the govern-ance partnership, which, in partnership or network governance arrange-ments, is essential to achieve both short and longer-term goals. However, there is substantial investment in community projects and indeed in com-munities and families, both in terms of funding and projects. While in terms of funding there is a large emphasis on communities, there are evi-dently unequal roles and power relations in the governance partnerships. The shadow of hierarchy operates within and through these structures, to reinforce this point: 'arrangements are not formed, nor do they operate, on a level playing field' (Marsh, 2011: 45). Embodying networks suggests that policy networks are able to examine and explain the relations, constraints and power relations on and between actors. Indeed, as Gains suggests, '(policy networks) highlight the power dependencies which arise from resource exchange and point to the importance of network integration in policy implementation' (Gains, 2003: 56).

Therefore, while Bevir and Rhodes suggest asymmetric critiques of part-nerships may place too much emphasis and indeed reify the role of the centre, their narrative emphasises the effect on the roles of the actors which make up the policy network or governance partnership in delivery. The roles and interpretation of the other partners' roles in governance and delivery of the rural renewal projects, is often contingent in renewal (both rural and urban) on the proximity to government of the actors, and par-ticularly, the large agencies often charged with oversight, funding and delivery by government. The focus on the USDA RD, as the governance agency responsible for decision making, as the key driver in the relations in the policy network, and the roles and relations between actors in terms of funding and delivery, suggest the role of the USDA RD as steering the gov-ernance partnership on behalf of the centre.

As Taylor (2000) notes, in hollowed out governance models the vital interaction is that which takes place between the centre and an actor, rather than between partners in collaborative delivery arrangements. This argument is one of resources and roles – how actors interpret the power they have and their role in delivery by their distance from the centre. Equally, Marsh (2011) suggests that to understand the role of actors and power relations across governance partnerships

[t]he DPM and APM in explaining actors' roles in the policy network, the role of structured inequality must be recognised. While Bevir and Rhodes (2006) emphasise that the shift from government to governance has resulted in a differentiated polity, that is, policies are the result of negotiated relations between competing actors in the policy network. Though Rhodes (2011), as noted earlier, insists that the DPM is intended to advance a neo-pluralist rather than pluralist arrangement, the emphasis on bargaining between actors in a segmented governance pattern has led critics to suggest this is too pluralistic an interpretation.

(Shand, 2013: 12–13)

The USDA RD is an excellent example of how major actors, often governance agencies, can shape agendas and roles in community engagement and can impose outcomes in both project delivery and the more complex machinations of governance – the USDA RD engaged with a range of partners such as businesses, healthcare, communities, and the ND RDC in North Dakota in delivery of projects. In terms of funding and the projects, this is illustrated not only by the role of the USDA RD as a partner in delivery. It is also illustrated by the importance of the USDA RD in governance, as discussed in earlier sections. The role of the USDA RD in governance is evidently central to the design and delivery of the rural renewal projects across North Dakota, but the organisation has worked with, as noted above, a range of actors, and the area's rural renewal in partnership.

Concluding remarks

This chapter has examined the key rural renewal projects across North Dakota. The focus of these is driven by key themes such as the development of businesses in the area, notably those of agriculture. However, the rural renewal programme also has a large focus on the development of other areas of infrastructure such as healthcare, transport and the communications network across North Dakota. These initiatives are related in terms of both short-term and longer-term outcomes, aimed at attracting people and business into the area and the longer-term investment in infrastructure through families, businesses and communities.

The projects focused upon in this chapter demonstrate the scope of rural renewal across North Dakota, but also the key themes of these efforts – healthcare, transport, housing, connectivity, and businesses development and community engagement. These underpinning aims are reflected in the governance of the rural renewal initiative across North Dakota and in the roles and power relations across the governance partnership in delivery. These are focused upon the role of the USDA RD as funder and decision maker in terms of awarding grants to competing projects. The effect of this role is evident across the actors in the governance partnership. The USDA RD as a key funder and driver of decision-making, funding conditions and gatekeeper in awarding funds shows the construction of roles in the governance partnership driven by the USDA RD on behalf of the national level.

The roles of other actors in the governance partnership are contingent upon the decisions made by the USDA RD and, as such, their own individual roles. The roles of the broader governance partnership in delivery of the rural renewal projects are driven by resources. The interaction and relations between actors is driven by the funding awarded and the gatekeeping attached to this. However, in applying aspects of interpretivism in the governance partnership, we see notions of political storytelling by large actors in the design of the rural renewal programme – which has implications for the roles of smaller actors in the governance partnership and in the delivery of the rural renewal projects across North Dakota. This is not a criticism of the major actors and funders, however, and the political storytelling is a narrative driven by investment in rural renewal infrastructure. To be sure, the funding and decision-making power and role of the USDA RD does shape the roles and relations of other actors in the North Dakota governance partnership, but the projects also draw on existing networks across the area involving farming and communities. In this way, as discussed in the analysis sections above, there is community engagement with the rural renewal projects and several amounts of funding supporting a broad range of rural renewal projects. The interaction of communities in the process of partnership, as discussed in the sections relating to the partnership governance model above, link to the notion of interactive governance in partnerships and networks. This role for the community in longer-term sustainability for infrastructure, business and connectedness for North Dakota is crucial to achieving the project's outcomes.

The role of communities in working with partners in the area and in realising the longer-term aims of the projects is the key to successful outcomes in rural renewal. Though dependent on the funding and conditions set by the larger government delivery actors, especially the USDA RD, the role of the community as key actors within the governance of rural renewal projects across North Dakota remains an essential part of connecting the development of public infrastructure, such as health, housing and transport, with the expansion of private sector expertise across North Dakota. This historical role of the community as a key actor in the governance and delivery of rural renewal in North Dakota, especially linked to the role of agriculture, healthcare and business development.

Key themes in North Dakota

- Funding and coordinating role of USDA RD
- Partnership focus emphasises community engagement role
- Community role also driven by ND RDC
- Projects focused on healthcare, connectivity, agriculture and business development

8 Relating theory to practice
Praxis, comparison and lesson drawing in governing rural renewal

Theory, practice and praxis: rural renewal and governance

This chapter examines the key themes of the book in terms of relating theory to practice – praxis, comparison and lesson drawing – and summarises these key themes from each case study area, across both theory and practice, summarising the contribution to the literature and to leadership and governance theory, as well as summarising the contribution to practice made by the book, and how these two contributions interlink. The chapter begins by examining the key themes of the rural renewal projects focused on in this book, drawn from the four case studies of the Vale of Glamorgan in the UK, NSW in Australia, North Dakota in the USA and the Eastern Cape in South Africa. The chapter then moves on to broaden these examples into a more general overview of rural renewal programmes, bringing in examples from European nations such as Ireland, and from East Asian examples like China. The chapter will then examine the key themes of rural renewal programmes which relate to theory and praxis, and where the relationship between theory and practice can be improved.

The governance of rural renewal: global comparison in theory and practice

Drawing on the governance of rural renewal globally, there are key themes in other case study examples which this book has not focused upon. These rural renewal programmes, such as examples in Ireland and China, each emphasise the role of communities and participation. The role of voluntary organisations and local businesses are also central to these rural renewal initiatives. The relationship between theory and practice in these examples, like the case study chapters examined in this book, demonstrates a partnership focus in governance design and delivery, made up of actors from different sectors. The projects focus on improving and developing areas such as housing, education and health, as well as transport infrastructure. In addition to this, the development of businesses, both in terms of building local businesses and growing agriculture and farming in these areas, are key themes of the projects, such as the development of sustainable food production and transportation. Examples of rural renewal programmes across different nations also show some commonalities with the case study areas focused on in this book. The key aspects of the partnerships – power relations, communication and the tension between leadership and coordination – are evident in the governance design and delivery in several examples of rural renewal programmes. Equally, the role of targets and resources are key aspects in the practice of rural renewal programmes, and are reflected in the underpinning frameworks of New Public Governance, aspects of NPM and policy networks.

However, there are also aspects of the rural renewal programmes that set out to combine more normative goals with targets. As we have seen in the Eastern Cape case study chapter, the projects aim to develop the existing tourism industry in the region, but also, in the longer term, to transform the identity of the region. Likewise, globally there are similar examples of tourism development driving rural renewal programmes. In China, for example, the area of Suzhou is undergoing rural renewal. The aims of the project are focused on the development of tourism and rural heritage in Suzhou. As Wang and Verdini (2012) argue, the role of heritage has long been central to urban tourism. In terms of rural renewal, however, the idea of heritage tourism is also an important factor. As Wang and Verdini (2012: 1) suggest:

> Rural tourism has been seen as a remedy for rural communities to combat the declining agrarian economy and diversify the multifunctional roles of agricultural land. In this trend toward agri-tourism, places of historical interests begin to take up an increasingly prominent role in rural regeneration ... places like these are of lesser significance so have a greater flexibility in making changes to their physical structures to meet contemporary needs, hence a greater potential to stimulate local economies and promote sustainable tourism with the involvement of local communities.
>
> (Wang and Verdini, 2012: 1)

In China, the government introduced a policy on rural development, Building New Countryside, involving the creation of new housing in rural areas. As Wang and Verdini (2012: 1) argue, the area of Suzhou City is one of cultural and historical significance:

> While the city has been dubbed the 'Venice of the East' its surrounding countryside is also characterised by canal-scape and features clusters of vernacular buildings and agriculture structures.
>
> (Wang and Verdini, 2012: 1)

Globally, agriculture and tourism are often drivers for rural renewal programmes. Similar to the Chinese example discussed above, the role of agritourism is also found in Canada. These key themes not only annotate consistencies across different rural renewal programmes globally, but also have implications for theory and practice. The linkage between government and business, particularly tourism and farming, makes the trend for partnership delivery more likely, raising once again key questions around the role of leadership, power relations, funding and communication, as well as the setting and achieving of targets and goals in the rural renewal programmes. In terms of theory, this strengthens the case for frameworks such as policy networks and New Public Governance, or multi-agency approaches. Reflexivity between theory and practice in this instance illustrates the enduring nature of targets and preponderance of partnership and network approaches to governance in rural renewal programmes. The Canadian example demonstrates the role of agritourism (with the development of an eco-museum and heritage tourism in rural renewal in the Saskatchewan region) and also emphasises the need to build international partnerships in delivering these goals for rural renewal. Examples such as this show these themes in practice, and each also exhibit aspects of the theoretical frameworks set out above. The following section now discusses these praxis elements with reference to the four case study areas of this book: the Vale of Glamorgan, North Dakota, the Eastern Cape and NSW.

Remaking governance through praxis?

There are a number of key aspects across the four cases that illustrate the notion of theory and practice. These vary in importance and emphasis in the cases, but can be thought of in the following categories:

* The role of communities
* Developing infrastructure
* Power relations
* Communication
* Leadership and coordination
* Funding and resources
* Partnership or network?

Taking each of these underpinning themes in turn, let us examine each of them with regard to the four case studies and also in terms of rural renewal programmes more generally (discussed with reference to other global examples elsewhere in this chapter).

Vale of Glamorgan, UK

- The role of communities: This case study shows real innovation in terms of community engagement. The community groups involved in the partnerships are in the main working with the local authority, farming bodies and voluntary groups.
- Developing infrastructure: Many of the rural renewal projects in the area focus on developing existing projects, such as transport links, employability, agricultural or education.
- Power relations: There are a large number of partners in the rural renewal projects, and several similar groups.
- Communication: The development of existing projects in the area has facilitated clear targets and understanding of roles.
- Leadership and coordination: Though there is some clear asymmetry in the governance delivery of the case study, with the local authority both leading and coordinating, there is a plurality of partners representing local businesses and community groups.
- Funding and resources: These are driven by the local authority and by local businesses.
- Partnership or network? In terms of governance design and delivery, the Vale of Glamorgan rural renewal partnership illustrates some asymmetry: the local authority is clearly the most powerful actor, and the wide range of local organisations and groups of more equal size and status show a larger degree of plurality. Moreover, there is also some degree of disaggregation in terms of delivery from the local authority to the local voluntary and community groups. This is facilitated by the development of existing projects and the important role of public service organisations such as schools. The rural renewal projects in the area are also heavily engaged with existing local businesses and voluntary groups. The role of voluntary groups and local businesses in the projects demonstrates the cross sectoral approach in the projects. The role of the local authority, as discussed in Chapter 4, is evidently emphasised as the major partner by the small scale of the rural renewal when compared to the other rural renewal cases in this book.

Eastern Cape, South Africa

- The role of communities: Community groups are engaged in the Nkonkobe and Alice rural renewal projects, as part of projects developing education, housing, and building civic and governmental infrastructure. Developing tourism and local businesses, as well as building a new identity as a vibrant educational centre.
- Developing infrastructure: This is focused on the development of civic and public life in the region, particularly around community

engagement and participation more broadly; also aimed at retaining talent in the region.

- Power relations: There is a clear power dynamic in the governance partnership, with the government departments and government agency driving the delivery and goals of the projects.
- Communication: There is a smaller number of actors in the partnership than in the UK case study, though these display much clearer differences in size and role.
- Leadership and coordination: The role of coordination is performed by the government agency on behalf of the government departments engaged in delivery of the projects.
- Funding and resources: The projects are, in the main, funded by the government agency and by the national bank.
- Partnership or network? The governance design and delivery in the Eastern Cape illustrates a partnership, with four major actors – the South African government agency, two government departments and a national bank, with smaller actors such as local and regional community groups, local businesses such as entrepreneurs, tourism and farming, and educational institutions from further and higher education.

NSW, Australia

- The role of communities: Communities are embedded in aspects of delivery such as agriculture and tourism.
- Developing infrastructure: There is a large focus on tourism and agricultural practice as a key driver for rural renewal in NSW
- Power relations: The FRRR is the largest delivery body in terms of rural renewal projects.
- Leadership and coordination: The FRRR drives large aspects of the governance model, both in terms of design, delivery and coordinating the programmes.
- Funding and resources: Again, the FRRR agency is a key driver in terms of funding and resource distribution, on behalf of regional and national government.
- Partnership or network? The governance model, despite being asymmetric and driven by the FRRR to a large extent, can still be described as a partnership; this is the aim of the design of rural renewal programme governance and though there are several actors engaged in delivery covering a range of sectors and projects, the governance model of delivery is too constrained to resemble a large-scale network.

North Dakota, USA

- The role of communities: Partners in governance?
- Developing infrastructure: Progress of projects.

- Power relations: Key actors in funding and delivery.
- Communication: Decision-making.
- Leadership and coordination: Power and decision making in delivering rural renewal.
- Funding and resources: Examining the flow of resources.
- Partnership or network? The relations in governance.

These key themes across the projects demonstrate findings which have resonance for theoretical approaches in governance. They also represent important learning examples for the practice and policy making of rural renewal.

The governance of rural renewal: the four case study areas in theory and practice

Drawing from the more general global examples of rural renewal programmes, the key issues which cut across theory and practice are also present in the four case study areas. This section examines each of the cases in terms of power relations, leadership and coordination, and outcomes.

First, the Vale of Glamorgan. Power relations in the rural renewal programme are widely dispersed. The main actor in the programme is the local authority, with a very diverse range of projects focused on tourism, agricultural business and education. The Vale of Glamorgan and the renewal of nearby Barry both emphasise the importance of engagement with local community and voluntary groups, and indeed seeks to support the work of these groups in existing ongoing projects, as well as to bring in new projects in the area. In terms of communication, this rural renewal programme is highly joined up; and in terms of power relations, highly disaggregated. It is a very pluralistic approach in design and delivery; obviously some asymmetries exist between the many partners engaged in delivery of rural renewal, as there is significant funding from the local authority. Though this funding aspect denotes a neo-pluralist power relationship among the local authority, the number of partners involved in the delivery of rural renewal projects in the Vale of Glamorgan indicates a very pluralistic governance design. The importance of the local level and the community in delivery and oversight of these projects in the Vale shows these to be key actors, drawing on national and (initially) supra national funding and rural renewal programmes.

The Eastern Cape rural renewal, focused in this book on Alice and Nkonkobe, has a smaller number of partners than the Vale of Glamorgan programme. The Eastern Cape shows a much more neo-pluralist approach, with lower levels of disaggregation of power. The roles of government agencies, departments and a national bank in funding and driving the rural renewal programmes demonstrate more central steering, and therefore, a different set of issues for praxis. Theoretically, the neo-pluralist aspect shows more asymmetry, less function given away, and a greater focus on targets as well as on partnership. In terms of relating these underpinning themes to practice, there are more hierarchical relations in the partnership (or network) and more leadership than coordination. The role of communities, in common with the other rural renewal programmes focused on in this book, is central to the aims of the programme concerned with the identity of the Alice region, transforming the area into a vibrant educational place. The relations between the partners in Alice and Nkonkobe show larger actors funding the programmes, working alongside resident communities and existing local businesses and voluntary organisations. There is a clear asymmetry in the partnership, with the larger actors funding the projects and also driving the aims and goals of these projects. As noted in Chapter 5, these involve setting targets some of these are longer term and more normative, such as the changing identity of the area and the improvement of infrastructure in the region.

Similarly, in the NSW case study, with such a large number of projects across a vast geographic area, the FRRR has adopted a more steering and leading role. Together with the funding of projects and the coordination and leadership of the partnership or network in these rural renewal projects, the FRRR is the largest partner, as the dedicated government agency. The FRRR's role is highly asymmetric, as there are distinct power differences between the actors. In terms of praxis, this neo-pluralist design addresses some of the key problems common across both theory and practice, but also raises different obstacles. The funding of projects from the agency solves potential issues of confusion or lack of direction around leadership, yet, in so doing, creates a highly top down structure with resource dependence from the other actors engaged in delivery. However, equally, in terms of communication, there is a clear direction in the projects, driven by a coordinated set of aims.

Turning to the North Dakota case study, the governance design and delivery of projects is similar to that of the NSW case. Equally, as one might expect, this has the same kinds of issues across theory and practice in terms of leadership, power relations and resource dependency, as well as targets and outcomes in the projects.

Why compare?

In setting out the general overview of rural renewal programmes and examples, like Ireland and China, the theme of comparison is broadened from the case study chapters. But why should we compare? First, the case studies focused on in this book are each different and the products of different contexts. As we have seen in each of the empirical chapters, the book has sought to compare across institutions, governance systems and design. For example, as discussed in Chapter 3, the community context is a significant influence on governance design in the respective cases. Comparing across the institutional design, in the federal and unitary cases (again, as discussed in more detail in Chapter 3), we see a more regional focus in the federal systems of the USA, Australia and South Africa. The much smaller and unitary (with some devolved powers and functions) UK case study of the Vale of Glamorgan shows a broader range of projects and a larger set of actors and partners engaged in the rural renewal projects. The UK case study also shows a far greater involvement of communities in the delivery of the projects when comparing with others. However, each of the case studies is evidently the product of its own historical and social context; for example, the need to integrate transport links in Eastern Cape and in NSW, while building agricultural business and housing infrastructure. Additionally, each of the case study areas sees different drivers for change –for example, the need to link urban and rural areas; the need to create identity; the need to ensure sustainable use of land and food – and these are goals across the case studies.

Governance approaches: revisiting theory to practice and practice to theory

The key themes discussed in this chapter relate to both theory and practice, emphasising the reflexivity of these themes such as the role of communities in governance. Drawing upon the four case studies focused on in this book, there are several key themes which are common across these cases, and which additionally have a more general resonance with rural renewal initiatives. These key themes are unpacked in the following sections, beginning with the question of partnerships in the governance of rural renewal, the central focus of the book.

Proliferation of partnerships: practice to theory?

Why have partnerships become such a ready-made answer to large regeneration projects? As we have seen in both Chapters 3 and the case study chapters, the idea of governance partnerships (or networks) has been used across a range of policy areas. From the UK experience, for example, the idea of joined-up government under the New Labour administration is one aspect of building partnerships, to generate cross-cutting responses to cross-cutting policy problems (which may involve education, voluntary services, communities, businesses, education etc.). However, in both rural and urban renewal programmes we see an adoption of partnerships: often, the partners are made up of local community groups, investment from SMEs or larger businesses, the voluntary sector, local or regional public services, government departments (national and local), and typically a dedicated (or specially created) governance agency which oversees the renewal initiative, as all or part of its remit. In the case study chapters, we have seen examples such as the FRRR in Australia and in the Nkonkobe projects in the Eastern Cape. As discussed in the overview of literature and debates in Chapter 2, there is much discussion of governance networks and partnerships in academic circles. But where did these ideas come from? While we can employ theoretical approaches such as policy networks (as indeed, this book does) or the New Public Governance, we need to revisit how such approaches have been driven by practice and policy examples. First, as noted in Chapter 2, the policy networks tradition evolved from scholarly research on government departments, annotating the shift from the Westminster model to a more differentiated, and subsequently asymmetric, mode of delivery (Rhodes, 1997; 2011). Likewise, the New Public Governance model describes the shift from NPM to a more agency-led, partnership mode of delivery as evidenced by the shift away from purely focusing on managerialism to a more multi-agency approach. Each of these frameworks has their roots in practice leading into theory, demonstrating the importance of both praxis and reflexivity in governance. This linkage and exchange relationship across theory and practice, however, shows several key themes across both theory and practice. The final chapter will examine each of these key themes, which we have seen in each of the four case study areas in this book, and indeed across several other rural renewal programmes.

9 Concluding remarks
Opportunities, challenges and next steps

This concluding chapter summarises the findings from the case studies and the broader discussion in the previous chapters. First, the chapter sets out the key findings from the case study areas in the rural renewal initiatives in the UK, Australia, South Africa and the USA in the Vale of Glamorgan, Nkonkobe, NSW and North Dakota. The first section of the chapter will touch upon some of the key themes which emerged from the findings and research questions. As the four case study chapters dealt with the key questions examined in the book, this concluding chapter will start by summarising the key themes arising from the four case study rural renewal programmes. The discussions of the findings will begin by looking at the key aspects which focus on design and delivery of the governance models. The sections below examine the findings in summary.

Summary of findings and research questions

1 Partners or networks: roles, power and who governs?
2 What is the role of communities in the rural renewal projects?
3 Who are the relevant stakeholders in the rural renewal projects?
4 Who drives funding and delivery in the rural renewal projects?
5 What is the sustainability of the rural renewal projects?

Partners or networks: roles, power and who governs?

The four cases illustrate, to varying degrees, the limits of partnership and networks in governance and delivery. To be sure, the issue of role construction and interpretation has consequences for how networks and partnerships operate. In the four rural renewal cases examined in this book, there are different roles in terms of which actors hold power, deliver function, and hold or require resources. The differing roles, as discussed in each of the case study chapters and in Chapter 3, did not show a great deal of influence on the programmes, suggesting the governance arrangements did indeed show many elements of partnerships – though asymmetric – rather than simply larger networks. The relations and differences in governance were evident though these did not prevent cooperation between the actors in delivery of the rural renewal programmes across the four case study areas.

What is the role of communities in the rural renewal projects?

Across the four case study areas, the role of communities is embedded in the governance of the rural renewal programmes. To be sure, the role of communities is a focus of the governance of each of the cases in terms of both design and delivery. These roles take place to varying extents and successes and are also linked to the success of the different actors and organisations engaged in governance in the cases. The central role of communities in the partnership arrangement is dependent to a large degree on external funding, as well as the aims of the projects and the extent of the existing development in the areas. This last point relates to the extent of industries such as tourism and farming, but also the development of the public or civic institutions in the case study area. Additionally, the sustainability of communities varies across the four rural renewal programmes – this is contingent on the geography of the cases as much as the governance. The development and sustainability of communities in the cases is also driven by the need to retain a critical mass of community, particularly talented younger people, in the areas. This also is embedded in the longer-term renewal of the cases in that the development and participation in these civic, educational or indeed private sector led organisations need to be attractive enough for a critical mass of talented young people to remain in the area. These people would then need to encourage other members of the community to participate in the development of these institutions, and to then attract other people to the area from outside and to remain there.

Who are the relevant stakeholders in the rural renewal projects?

The four rural renewal programmes are each driven by a series of co-operating stakeholders, as we have seen throughout this book. However, the relevant stakeholders can be thought of as those who participate in, and who coordinate, the projects. This is a separate set of issues to the following question around funding and delivery, as there are several actors in the cases who drive participation and make the rural renewal projects visible and connected to the existing activity in the area. For example, there are several examples of small businesses in the Vale of Glamorgan case study which demonstrate the need for existing vehicles for development, which the local community are already connected with, to buy into the aims of the rural renewal programme.

Who drives funding and delivery in the rural renewal projects?

These actors may seem to be more on the periphery of the design of the renewal programmes (as they are already successful) but are vital in connecting people to the aims of the projects. The need for community awareness in achieving any type of renewal is essential, whether rural or urban, in a large-scale or small-scale project. The incumbent organisations – public, private or voluntary – in the area need to be involved or at least aware of the aims of the project, whatever the extent they are engaged in shaping these.

What is the sustainability of the rural renewal projects?

Across the projects, the need for sustainability is a core aim. Key aspects of sustainability are embedded in the design and delivery of the four rural renewal programmes. However, given the broad and contested nature of sustainability and sustainable development as concepts, these are obviously difficult to unite across four different case studies in four different countries. Accepting this, there are some shared traits of sustainability in the rural renewal programmes. These can be thought of in three distinct ways. First, the notion of economic and financial sustainability; second, the idea of ecological and planning sustainability; and third, the idea of community driven sustainability. The third aspect is termed community, as this is a common theme across the cases, rather than the broader and more traditional use of the term social sustainability. In addition, these themes owe as much to the more recent idea of the triple crunch as to the more established notion of the three pillars or triple bottom line. This is due to the role of resources in each of the case study areas. Resources scarcity and protection remains, evidently, a vital issue and one that drives the land management in rural renewal. Let us discuss each of the three aspects of sustainability in turn. First, that of financial sustainability:

i Financial sustainability

In each of the four case studies, there is an emphasis on job creation and business development. While this is not unusual in any renewal programme, the rural focus of the cases is reflected in the types of industry, employment and development. For example, the rural renewal programmes examined here share common elements, as noted elsewhere in this book. The commonalities of industry, focused on the development of tourism, agriculture and existing enterprise in the four cases do have different implications for renewal than many other larger projects; these key difference are also grounded in the rural rather than urban focus of the four cases. Again, the commonalities across rural renewal cases around financial sustainability are markedly different from the financial planning and development aspects of urban renewal programmes. For example, the focus in our rural cases is to develop existing community driven businesses to generate employment and business development as a priority, rather than solely seek to attract outside investment from larger, global established companies. Equally, this strategy is tied to the development of community development – the development of locally grown businesses is intended to attract people to the area. Additionally, the growth of businesses across the four rural renewal areas is tied to the community, particularly through agriculture and land management. The local knowledge harnessed in these endeavours requires attracting people to stay or to join the community. To be sure, there is a large role evident across the four cases for developing public life – there is not a focus on public or private but rather the development of both businesses and civic institutions in the case study areas. The linkage in terms of financial sustainability is clearly not one reliant on a large amount of outward investment from larger global corporates, but rather one of developing existing profit making enterprises in the areas and linking the growth of public participation and the growth of communities to the development of public life and private growth. The financial sustainability of the rural renewal initiatives is characterised across the four cases by the need to make sure the programmes are not reliant on government (or governance agency) funding in the longer term, but instead the programmes embed the development of income streams and sustainable communities and participation, both in terms of enabling businesses to grow profit, and in growing the size of the community to drive and develop infrastructure and a solid sustainable base of residents in the area.

ii Ecological sustainability

The role of land use in the four rural renewal case studies is an important one. Most evidently, the need to develop rural land is a sensitive debate, but the aims in the rural renewal cases examined here demonstrate the development of land through agriculture – such as the management of land in NSW – and the linkage between rural and urban communities in Nkonkobe in the Eastern Cape. The role of land use and planning, and connecting the rural and urban, also underpins key aspects of the Vale of Glamorgan and North Dakota cases. The focus of agriculture and developing this in the case studies links the financial, ecological and community elements of sustainability and sustainable development.

iii Sustainable communities

Across each of the four rural renewal case study areas, there is a large focus on the engagement of communities with the projects. This is focused on both the short and longer term, and particularly in growing the community in the life of the area through businesses, civic participation, and growing identity. The notion of sustainable communities is one that is widely set out in rural (and urban) renewal programmes, in both large and small projects. The issue that each of our four rural renewal case studies face is the need to retain younger, talented people in the area. Related to this, there is a need – evidenced by the focus on tourism in the cases – to attract people to the area to holiday and to work. As noted in Chapter 2, there is not room or focus in this book to examine fully the sustainable tourism literature, but the development of these industries in the rural renewal projects examined in this book is a key theme in achieving the aims of the four programmes.

Governing as leading or coordinating: what have we learnt?

This focus of the partnership or network approach to governance in large-scale renewal initiatives (both rural and urban) and drawing on the cases examined in this book, illustrates the focus of collaboration between actors. Within such partnership arrangements in governance, there are evidently elements of power and communication. Drawing on the interpretivist perspective, this book examines the ways in which leadership and governance processes function, applying the notion of leaders understanding their roles in relation to the ways they construct meaning around other leaders and their roles in relation to their own (Mead, 1934; Bevir, 2009). Revisiting the steering and rowing debate, we can see that within partnerships there are issues which arise in terms of the coordination and leadership of the partners (or broader network). For example, as we have seen in the four case study chapters, the partners engaged in the rural renewal initiatives are not from the same sector; nor are they the same size or possessed of the same financial resources. Within the partnerships, therefore, we see a range of issues such as *power*. The power relations between the partners may be asymmetric or more equal in nature, but the differences in power between actors in the partnership can lead to other consequences for the partnerships and the projects. First, the power relations between partners may affect *communication*. As discussed with reference to role construction in the case study chapters, communication between the actors is affected by power relations, and related issues such as funding or resources. The issues of *outcomes and value for money* in the projects are still focused on the results across various areas, such as increasing levels of housing, raising educational attainment, or increasing levels of employment in the rural renewal programmes. Of course, there are more normative and less measurable goals in the case study areas such as the creation and development of sustainable communities and developing a sense of identity and place in the areas, such as the Alice regeneration strategy in the Eastern Cape examined in Chapter 6.

New public management: Though we have seen a shift in theory towards New Public Governance from NPM, in practice we still see enduring elements of NPM across the four case study areas. The role of targets remains important in the rural renewal projects, whether these are short term or longer term, such as house building and job creation, or expanding the role of tourism or agricultural business. The role of theory and practice linkage requires unpacking here. Though elements of NPM, such as an emphasis on outcomes, has been fused to an extent with partnership or network delivery in governance, demonstrating aspects of New Public Governance, in practice contexts there is not such a smooth transition or discussion. The projects in the case study areas each display elements of NPM, such as a focus on targets and outcomes. Though we see an over-riding emphasis on partnerships and networks, we also see a combination of NPM and New Public Governance. The issue of reflexivity, discussed by Rhodes (1997), emphasises both theory learning from practice, and practice from theory. As we have seen, the key aspects of the partnership relate both to academic circles and the rural renewal programmes.

The role of governance agencies: The role of governance agencies, created by successive governments, has proved confusing and problematic and frustrated delivery of public services. This design and delivery failure has led to enduring issues of mistrust, accusations of cronyism, and governance failures in designing and delivery policy. Both in the public and private sectors, hyperactive or confusing delivery mechanisms add to perceptions of overly bureaucratic structures and have led to rapid change in central government targets, which have global and comparative relevance, and to the centrality of multi-agency working. Such changes have left the public and many corporate or public sector actors unengaged in the governance process.

Rural renewal and governance design: In each of the case studies, the private sector – and particularly small existing businesses in the regions – is a vital player in debates around public and private design and provision. This design of governance is underpinned by overlapping and complementary agencies in the partnership structures, with distinctions between the public and private, and between communities. The idea of cooperation and the role of design and delivery across the public and private sectors means the need to pay attention to future design of these instruments.

Governance design and instruments: Examining the key lessons from the case studies evaluates, across the cases and more broadly, how the projects and arrangements between the actors are designed. These need to ensure cooperation between these actors, avoiding a drift towards a neo-pluralist design or to models which resemble governance arrangements which are suited to neither public, private nor partnership models.

Linking the research to the broader debates and literatures

This book contributes to a number of literatures, chiefly those of Public Policy and Comparative Public Policy, and more broadly through themes of governance, power and the role of government, to aspects of Comparative Politics debates. In addition, the research also has implications for Planning literatures given the role of housing and land use in some of the key aims across the four rural renewal case studies examined here. Allied to each of these discipline areas, the various and many areas of sustainability literature also relate to several of the key themes of this book and the four rural renewal cases examined within it. These are themes such as the use of resources – both in terms of the triple bottom line and the triple crunch, but also, and equally fundamentally for the rural renewal projects across the four cases – the implications for funding and sustainability, and the related involvement of communities and business in the rural renewal process. To be sure, each of the projects in the Vale of Glamorgan, the Eastern Cape, in NSW and in North Dakota displays high levels of community involvement both in design and in implementation, and this is intended to embed local benefits and development over a longer time period, ensuring the sustainability of the renewal projects. Evidently, renewal programmes are designed with both short and longer-term goals in mind, and in terms of rural renewal and our four cases in this book, this is a delicate balance to achieve. For example, each case study attempts to ensure the expansion and development (and protection) of agricultural trade in the area in the short term and also plan for the future. Similarly, in terms of tourism, each of the case study areas identifies the need to develop existing success and businesses in the tourism industry. The financial sustainability of these endeavours is obviously crucial, but longer term, will need to operate successfully without the need of a dedicated government agency to drive funding and coordinate partnerships in order to deliver successful outcomes. The role of communities will evidently be central to achieving a successful tourism model in each of the four rural renewal case studies, as the need to anchor community roles in both civic and business life in the areas over the longer term will allow development and generation of income, while also generating jobs and further employment for local communities. This focus, in many cases, notably the Nkonkobe rural renewal programme in the Eastern Cape case, as we saw in Chapter 6, was implemented alongside plans to grow other aspects (though which would also relate to attracting people to the region) of renewal, such as public and community institutions with the aim of attracting younger people to stay in the area and participate in its growth, as well as expanding the university in the area. This illustrates the joined-up focus of rural (like urban) renewal, and is reflected in its governance in several instances. The book contributes to the public policy, governance and policy networks literature. The book also contributes to the fields of comparative public policy and politics. The contribution of the book to these different areas of academic debates, and also to the practical and policy aspects of regeneration and governance, has been drawn from the four rural regeneration initiatives of the Vale of Glamorgan, The Eastern Cape focused on Nkonkobe, NSW and North Dakota. It is to the topic of possible further research that the next section turns.

Further research

In terms of further research, there are several different types of renewal project, both in rural and urban settings, and in a variety of geographical settings, local, regional and national. The context of regeneration tends to vary greatly between these projects leaving much scope for further research. Evidently, each of these programmes of renewal requires some system of governance and, further to this, the governance systems employed to deliver the renewal programmes tend to be couched within existing institutional systems, and so are driven by federal or unitary, regional or devolved arrangements. We have also seen, in both rural and urban renewal programmes, the creation of large agencies decentralised from central government departments with responsibility to fund and deliver the renewal programs, often, as we have seen in this book and elsewhere (Shand, 2013), as part of a larger partnership or network of actors representing differing groups or sectors. Conceptually, as argued in this book, we still see the focus on targets and effectiveness from New Public Management, though couched in the partnership-focused delivery of New Public Governance. Equally, these delivery mechanisms are underpinned by the interpretive notion of governance – the behaviour of the actors in delivery is reflected by their views of their own roles and those of each other.

In terms of practice, each of these arrangements has implications in terms of power, resources, and decision making. Underpinning these themes, there are also issues around coordination and leadership, as well as the allocation of budgets. To this end, the extent of decentralisation is still driven by agencies delivering projects on behalf of government departments. The broad meaning and application of the term and idea of renewal (regeneration, aspects of rural and/or urban development) also means that it is applied to a great range of areas and projects, each of which have value as further research case studies. For example, the role of events or mega city projects, often driven by cultural or sporting events (such as Olympics, Commonwealth or other global events such as football world cups), have implications for the scale and aims of the renewal programme (whether rural or urban). Additionally, further research areas could be focused around themes such as faith, art, or the role of the voluntary sector in renewal, both rural and urban.

Concluding remarks

Though the existing literature in the governance and politics field (and related areas such as human geography) addresses some of these points in terms of the governance of regeneration, there is no real national-level comparison across countries which focuses on the role of the third sector in governance. While there is some highly detailed and excellent work at the national and sub-national level on the topic (Osborne *et al.*, 2002, 2004; Long and Woods, 2011) and some comparative analysis at the national level from a governance perspective, this is not comparative in a global sense. Therefore, the book sets out to build on and contribute to the debates fostered by the existing literature in academic circles and in practice, but also seeks to build on this in two main ways: (i) by broadening existing academic and practice debates on the governance of regeneration to a cross-national comparative level, focused on communities, governments and businesses, and (ii) to link these debates in more depth to the much larger existing body of work on governance of urban regeneration. Additionally, of course, there are several types of land use in renewal programmes. Each of these provide several opportunities for greyfield (land which is a mixture of new and previously used sites) renewal, as we have seen in some Australian programmes, for greenfield development as part of a regeneration initiative (which often includes a focus on community and environmental development) or for brownfield renewal which focuses on development of previously used sites, often for community, transport or housing facilities. As we have seen in this book, there are several examples of previously used buildings or land being used for community or civic renewal projects.

In the South African case study of Nkonkobe, the community may manage projects and work with private sector providers, but the funding for such initiatives is, in the main, provided by the national and regional tiers of governance. As examined throughout this book, across the four case studies, the focus on partnerships in design and delivery of the governance involves overlapping tiers in policy delivery between federal and local levels (for example, in NSW and North Dakota), as well as delivery in the programmes driven by decentralised governance agencies, voluntary and community groups and the existing private sector.

References

Alcock, P. (2011) 'Constituting the Third Sector: Processes of Decontestation and Contention Under the UK Labour Governments in England'. *International Journal of Voluntary and Nonprofit Organisations*, 22 (3): 450–469.

Alice Regeneration Programme – High Level Feasibility Assessment Report (2010) National Treasury of South Africa and ASPIRE. Available online at: www.aspire. org.za/reports/Alice%20Regeneration%20-%20High%20Level%20Feasibility %20Assessment%20-%20Final.pdf

Amathole District Municipality Land Reform and Settlement Plan (2003). Available online at: www.amathole.gov.za/old/attachments/article/324/FINAL%20 IDP%202012-2017.pdf

Bennett, P., Delorey, R., Oland, K. and Yuill, C. (2013) *Pathway to Rural Regeneration: Transforming Small Schools into Community Hubs*. Nova Scotia Small Schools Initiative: Nova Scotia Commission on the New Economy.

Bevir, M. (2004) 'Governance and Interpretation: What are the Implications of Postfoundationalism?' *Public Administration*, 82 (3): 605–625.

Bevir, M. (2009) *Key Concepts in Governance*. London: Sage Publications Ltd.

Bevir, M. (2010) 'Interpreting Territory and Power'. *Government and Opposition*, 45 (3): 436–456.

Bevir, M. (2011) 'Public Administration as Storytelling'. *Public Administration*, 89 (1): 183–195.

Bevir, M. (2012) *Governance: A Very Short Introduction*. Oxford: Oxford University Press.

Bevir, M. (ed.) (2013) *The Sage Handbook of Governance*. London: Sage Publications Ltd.

Bevir, M. and Rhodes, R. (2003) 'Comparative Governance: Prospects and Lessons'. *Public Administration* 81 (1): 191–210.

Bevir, M. and Rhodes, R. (2004a) 'Interpretation as Method, Explanation, and Critique: A Reply'. *British Journal of Politics and International Relations*, 6: 156–161.

Bevir, M. and Rhodes, R. (2004b) 'Interpreting British Governance'. *British Journal of Politics and International Relations*, 6: 130–136.

Bevir, M. and Rhodes, R. (2006) 'Interpretive Approaches to British Government and Politics'. *British Politics* 1: 84–112.

Bevir, M. and Rhodes, R. (2008) 'The Differentiated Polity as Narrative'. *British Journal of Politics and International Relations*, 10 (4): 729–734.

Bevir, M. and Rhodes, R. (2011) 'The stateless state', in M. Bevir (ed.) *The Sage Handbook of Governance* (pp. 203–217). London: Sage Publications Ltd.

Bevir, M. and Rhodes, R. (2012) 'Interpretivism and the analysis of traditions and practices'. *Critical Policy Studies*, 6 (2): 85–99.

Bevir, M. and Richards, D. (2009a) 'Decentring Policy Networks: A Theoretical Agenda'. *Public Administration*, 87 (1): 3–14.

Bevir, M. and Richards, D. (2009b) 'Decentring Policy Networks: Lessons and Prospects'. *Public Administration*, 87 (1): 132–141.

Bhuyan, S. and Olson, E. (1998) 'Potential role of non-agricultural cooperatives in rural development: A report on focus group studies conducted in rural North Dakota'. Available online at: ageconsearch.umn.edu

Borzel, T. (1998) 'Organising Babylon: On the different conceptions of Policy Networks'. *Public Administration* 76 (2): 253–273.

Borzel, T. (2003) 'Networks: Reified Metaphor or Governance Panacea?' *Public Administration*, 89 (1): 49–63.

Catney, P. Dixon, T. and Henneberry, J. (2000) 'Hyperactive Governance in the Thames Gateway'. *Journal of Urban Regeneration and Renewal*, 2 (2): 122–145.

Cordes, S. (1989) 'The Changing Rural Environment and the Relationship between Health Services and Rural Development'. *Health Services Research*, 23 (6): 757–784.

Davies, J. (2002) 'The Governance of Urban Regeneration: A Critique of the "Governing without Government" Thesis'. *Public Administration*, 80 (2): 301–322.

Davies, J. S. (2005) 'Local Governance and the Dialectics of Hierarchy, Market and Network'. *Policy Studies*, 26 (3–4): 311–335.

Davies, J. S. (2009) 'The Limits of Joined-Up Government: Towards a Political Analysis'. *Public Administration*, 87 (1): 80–96.

Department of Agriculture and Rural Development, Rural Development Programme. Available online at: www.dardni.gov.uk/index/rural-development-programme

Dolowitz, D. and Marsh, D. (1996) 'Who Learns What from Whom: a Review of the Policy Transfer Literature'. *Political Studies*, XLIV 343–357.

Dolowitz, D. and Marsh, D. (2000) 'Learning from Abroad: The Role of Policy Transfer in Contemporary Policy-Making'. *Governance*, 13 (1): 5–23.

Dowding, K. (1995) 'Model or Metaphor? A Critical Review of the Policy Network Approach'. *Political Studies*, 43 (1): 136–158.

Dowding, K. (2001) 'There Must Be End to Confusion: Policy Networks, Intellectual Fatigue, and the Need for Political Science Methods Courses in British Universities'. *Political Studies*, 49: 89–105.

Eastern Cape Rural Development Agency (2010). Available online at: www.ecrda.co.za

Eastern Cape's Provincial Growth and Development Plan (2008). Available online at: www.ecsecc.org/files/library/documents/PGDP_Assessment_2008.pdf

Edwards, B., Goodwin, M., Pemberton, S. and Woods, M. (2000) *Partnership Working In Rural Regeneration: Governance and Empowerment*. Bristol and York: Policy Press and Joseph Rowntree Foundation.

Elazar, D. (1997) 'Contrasting Federal and Unitary Systems'. *International Political Science Review*, 18 (3): 237–251.

Elgie, R. (2011) 'Core Executive Studies Two Decades On'. *Public Administration*, 89 (1): 64–77.

Foundation for Rural and Regional Renewal (2010) *Rural Education Report.* Available online at: www.frrr.org.au/resources/157a_FRRR%20REP%20Report%202010%20(2).pdf

Foundation for Rural and Regional Renewal (2010) *Evaluation of Performance Over the First Ten Years and the Contribution the FRRR Makes to Rural and Regional Australia.* Available online at www.frrr.org.au/resources/FRRR%20Marketing%20Report%20Brief%20Final%20with%20TFFF.pdf

Gains, F. (2003) 'Executive Agencies in Government: The Impact of Bureaucratic Networks on Policy Outcomes'. *Journal of Public Policy,* 23 (1): 55–73.

Gains, F. and Stoker, G. (2011) 'Special advisers and the transmission of ideas from the policy primeval soup'. *Policy & Politics,* 39 (4): 485–498.

Gallent, N. and Robinson, S. (2012) Community Perspectives on Localness and 'Priority' Housing Policies in Rural England. *Housing Studies,* 27 (3): 360–380.

Geertz, C. (1993) *The Interpretation of Cultures: Selected Essays.* London: Fontana.

Herbert-Cheshire, L. (2000) 'Contemporary Strategies for Rural Community Development In Australia: A Governmentality Perspective'. *Journal of Rural Studies,* 16 (2): 203–215.

Herbert-Cheshire, L. (2004) 'From Risky to Responsible: Expert Knowledge and the Governing of Community-Led Rural Development'. *Journal of Rural Studies,* 20 (3): 289–303.

Hood, C. (1991) 'A Public Management for All Seasons?' *Public Administration,* 69 (1): 3–19.

Hood, C. (2011) 'It's Public Administration, Rod, but Maybe Not As We Know It: British Public Administration in the 2000s'. *Public Administration,* 89 (1): 128–139.

Howell, K. E. (2013) *The Philosophy of Methodology.* London: Sage Publications Ltd.

James, O. and Lodge, M. (2003) 'The Limitations of "Policy Transfer" and "Lesson Drawing" for Public Policy Research'. *Political Studies Review,* 1: 179–193.

Kort, M. and Klijn, E. (2012) 'Public-Private Partnerships in Urban Regeneration: Democratic Legitimacy and its Relation with Performance and Trust'. *Local Government Studies,* 39 (1): 89–106.

Kjær, A. M. (2004) *Governance.* Cambridge: Polity Press.

Kjær, A. M. (2011) 'Rhodes' Contribution TO Governance Theory: Praise, Criticism AND The Future Governance Debate'. *Public Administration,* 89 (1): 101–113.

Liddle, J. and Diamond, J. (2007) 'Reflections on Regeneration Management Skills Research'. *Public Money and Management,* 27 (3): 189–192.

Long, H. L. and Woods, M. (2011) 'Rural restructuring under globalization in eastern coastal China: What can be learned from Wales'. *Journal of Rural and Community Development,* 6 (1): 70–94.

March, J. G. and Olsen, J. P. (1984) 'The New Institutionalism: Organizational Factors in Political Life'. *The American Political Science Review,* 78 (3): 734–749.

Marsh, D. (2008) 'What is at Stake? A Response to Bevir and Rhodes'. *British Journal of Politics and International Relations,* 10 (4): 735–739.

Marsh, D. (2011) 'The New Orthodoxy: The Differentiated Polity Model'. *Public Administration,* 89 (1): 32–48.

Marsh, D. and Rhodes, R. (1992) *Policy Networks in British Government*. Oxford: Clarendon Press.

Marsh, D. and Smith, M. (2000) 'Understanding Policy Networks: towards a Dialectical Approach'. *Political Studies* 48: 4–21.

Marsh, D., Richards, D. and Smith, M. (2003) 'Unequal Plurality: Towards an Asymmetric Power Model of British Politics'. *Government and Opposition*, 38 (3): 306–332.

Matthews, P. and O'Brien, D. (2015) *After Urban Regeneration*. Bristol: Policy Press.

Mead, G. H. (1934) *Mind, Self and Society: From the Standpoint of a Social Behaviorist*. Morris, C. W. (ed.). Chicago and London: The University of Chicago Press.

Nature Conservation Council National Conference 2015. Available online at: www.nature.org.au/healthy-ecosystems/bushfire-program/conferences/

Nkonkobe Spatial Development Framework (2004). Available online at: www.nkonkobe.gov.za/?q=system/files/filedepot/2/IDP%202014_15.pdf

Odagiri, T. (2011) *Rural Regeneration in Japan*. Centre for Rural Economy Research Report. University of Newcastle upon Tyne.

Osborne, S. (2006) 'The New Public Governance?' *Public Management Review*, 8 (3): 377–387.

Osborne, S. (ed.) (2010) *The New Public Governance? Emerging Perspectives On the Theory and Practice of Public Governance*. Abingdon and New York: Routledge.

Osborne, S. P. and Brown, L. (2011) 'Innovation, Public Policy and Public Services Delivery in the UK. The word that would be king?' *Public Administration*, 89 (4): 1335–1350.

Osborne, S., Beattie, R. and Williamson, A. (2002) *Community involvement in rural regeneration partnerships in the UK: Evidence from England, Northern Ireland and Scotland*. Bristol: Policy Press.

Osborne, S., Beattie, R. and Williamson, A. (2004) 'Community Involvement in Rural Regeneration Partnerships: Exploring the Rural Dimension'. *Local Government Studies*, 30 (2): 156–181.

Rhodes, R. (1996) 'The New Governance: Governing Without Government'. *Political Studies*, 44 (4): 652–667.

Rhodes, R. (1997) *Understanding Governance: Policy Networks, Governance, Reflexivity, and Accountability*. Buckingham: Open University Press.

Rhodes, R. (2007) 'Understanding Governance: Ten Years On'. *Organization Studies*, 28 (8): 1243–1264.

Rose, R. (1991) 'What is Lesson Drawing?' *Journal of Public Policy*, 11 (1): 3–30.

Shand, R. (2013) *Governing Sustainable Urban Renewal: Partnerships in Action*. Abingdon: Routledge.

Smith, M. (1999) *The Core Executive in Britain*. London: St. Martin's Press.

Sorensen, E. (2002) 'Democratic Theory and Network Governance'. *Administrative Theory and Praxis*, 24 (4): 693–720.

Sorensen, E. (2012) 'Governance Networks as a Frame for Inter-Demoi Participation and Deliberation'. *Administrative Theory and Praxis*, 34 (4): 509–532.

Sorensen, E. (2013) 'Institutionalizing Interactive Governance for Democracy'. *Critical Policy Studies*, 7 (1): 72–86.

Stockdale, A. (2006) 'Migration: Pre-requisite for Rural Economic Regeneration?' *Journal of Rural Studies*, 22 (3): 354–366.

Stoker, G. (1998) 'Governance as Theory: Five Propositions'. *International Social Science Journal*, 50 (155): 17–28.

Stoker, G. (2006) 'Public Value Management: A New Narrative for Networked Governance?' *American Review of Public Administration*, 36 (1): 41–57.

Stone, D. (2000) 'Non-Governmental Policy Transfer: The Strategies of Independent Policy Institutes'. *Governance*, 13 (1): 45–70.

Sullivan, H. (2011) *Performing Governance*. Basingstoke: Palgrave MacMillan.

Taylor, A (2000) 'Hollowing Out or Filling In? Taskforces and the Management of Cross Cutting Issues in British Government'. *British Journal of Politics and International Relations*, 2 (1): 46–71.

The Comprehensive Spending Review (2010). London: HM Treasury.

USDA Rural Development Healthcare, 2014. Available online at: www.rd.usda.gov/files/RD2014ProgressReport.pdf

Vale of Glamorgan Local Development Plan (LDP) 2011–2026 (2013). Available online at: www.valeofglamorgan.gov.uk/Documents/Living/Planning/Policy/LDP-2013/01-LDP-Deposit-Plan-Written-Statement-2013.pdf

Welsh Government (2010) *Economic Renewal: A New Direction*. Available online at: www.wlga.gov.uk/download.php?id=3971&l=1

Welsh Government (2006) *Environment Strategy for Wales*. Available online at: http://gov.wales/topics/environmentcountryside/epq/envstratforwales/?lang=en

Welsh Government (2008) *The Wales Spatial Plan*. Available online at: www.torfaen.gov.uk/cy/Related-Documents/Forward-Planning/SD78-PeoplePlaces Futures-TheWalesSpatialPlan2008Update.pdf

Welsh Government (2008) *The Wales Transport Strategy*. Available online at: http://gov.wales/docs/det/publications/140909-transport-strategy-en.pdf

Welsh Government (2010) *Economic Renewal: A New Direction*. Available online at: www.wlga.gov.uk/download.php?id=3971&l=1

Wolman, H. (1992) 'Understanding cross national policy transfers: the case of Britain and the US'. *Governance*, 5 (1): 27–45.

Woods, N. (2002) 'Global governance and the role of institutions'. *Governing globalization: Power, authority and global governance*: 25–45.

Index

Page numbers in *italics* denote tables, those in **bold** denote figures.